INSTRUCTIONS FOR LIVING

THE TEN COMMANDMENTS

Edited by
ED GALLAGHER

Instructions for Living: The Ten Commandments

Published by Heritage Christian University Press

Copyright © 2018, 2021 by Ed Gallagher

Manufactured in the United States of America

Cataloging-in-Publication Data

Instructions for living: the Ten Commandments / edited by Ed Gallagher

p. cm.

Berean Study Series

Includes scripture index.

ISBN 978-1-956811-02-5 (pbk.) 978-1-956811-03-2 (ebook)

1. Ten Commandments. I. Gallagher, Edmon, L. editor. II. Title. III. Series.

241.52—dc20

Library of Congress Control Number: 2021920234

Cover design by Brad McKinnon and Brittany Vander Maas.
All rights reserved. No part of this publication may be reproduced, distributed, stored in a retrieval system, or transmitted in any form or by any means without the prior written permission of the publisher, except in the case of brief quotations embodied in critical reviews and certain other noncommercial uses permitted by copyright law.

For information:
Heritage Christian University Press
3625 Helton Drive
PO Box HCU
Florence, AL 35630

www.hcu.edu

CONTENTS

Bible Abbreviations — v

1. INTRODUCING THE TEN COMMANDMENTS — 1
   Ed Gallagher

2. THE CHRISTIAN AND OLD TESTAMENT LAW — 12
   Nathan Daily

3. I AM THE LORD YOUR GOD — 25
   Jeremy Barrier

4. NO OTHER GODS — 32
   W. Kirk Brothers

5. NO IDOLS — 42
   Arvy Dupuy

6. THE NAME OF THE LORD — 50
   Bill Bagents

7. KEEPING THE SABBATH — 58
   C. Wayne Kilpatrick

8. HONORING PARENTS — 65
   Philip Goad

9. AGAINST MURDER — 73
   Brad McKinnon

10. AGAINST ADULTERY — 81
    Michael Jackson

11. AGAINST STEALING — 90
    Matt Heupel

12. AGAINST LYING — Travis Harmon — 97

13. AGAINST COVETING — Justin Guin — 105

Bibliography — 115
Scripture Index — 119
Credits — 126
Contributors — 128
Berean Study Series — 132

BIBLE ABBREVIATIONS

Old Testament

Gen	Genesis
Exod	Exodus
Lev	Leviticus
Num	Numbers
Deut	Deuteronomy
Josh	Joshua
Judg	Judges
Ruth	Ruth
1–2 Sam	1–2 Samuel
1–2 Kgs	1–2 Kings
1–2 Chr	1–2 Chronicles
Ezra	Ezra
Neh	Nehemiah
Esth	Esther
Job	Job
Ps	Psalms
Prov	Proverbs

Eccl	Ecclesiastes
Song	Song of Solomon
Isa	Isaiah
Jer	Jeremiah
Lam	Lamentations
Ezek	Ezekiel
Dan	Daniel
Hos	Hosea
Joel	Joel
Amos	Amos
Obad	Obadiah
Jonah	Jonah
Mic	Micah
Nah	Nahum
Hab	Habakkuk
Zeph	Zephaniah
Hag	Haggai
Zech	Zechariah
Mal	Malachi

New Testament

Matt	Matthew
Mark	Mark
Luke	Luke
John	John
Acts	Acts
Rom	Romans
1–2 Cor	1–2 Corinthians
Gal	Galatians

Eph	Ephesians
Phil	Philippians
Col	Colossians
1–2 Thess	1–2 Thessalonians
1–2 Tim	1–2 Timothy
Titus	Titus
Phlm	Philemon
Heb	Hebrews
Jas	James
1–2 Pet	1–2 Peter
1–2–3 John	1–2–3 John
Jude	Jude
Rev	Revelation

1. INTRODUCING THE TEN COMMANDMENTS

ED GALLAGHER

MATTHEW 22:37–40

One Main Thing

Throughout history and still today the Ten Commandments have served as a helpful summary of what God expects from his people.

Introduction

On the plains of Moab outside the Promised Land, Moses reminded the people of Israel about what had happened decades earlier when they arrived at Mt. Sinai:

> You came near and stood at the base of the mountain, a mountain blazing with fire into the heavens and enveloped in a totally black cloud.

> Then the Lord spoke to you from the fire. You kept hearing the sound of the words, but didn't see a form; there was only a voice. He declared his covenant to you. He commanded you to follow the Ten Commandments, which he wrote on two stone tablets. (Deut 4:11–13)

This retelling of the Sinai narrative that readers first encounter in Exodus 19–20 highlights the special importance of the Ten Commandments, the first rules that God spoke directly to the people and wrote himself on two stone tablets. In Deuteronomy, Moses goes on to remind the people of what these Ten Commandments are (ch. 5), an account that corresponds to the original giving of these commandments in Exodus 20:1–17. Though Jewish tradition finds 613 commandments in the entire Torah,[1] these ten stand out as having special importance.

Going Deeper

We know that the Ten Commandments are important for a number of reasons. First of all, they appear twice as a group in Scripture (Exod 20; Deut 5). Secondly, they are the first and most important commandments in the Torah, judging by their unique status as inscribed on stone tablets by God's own hand.[2] In this way, it seems that these Ten Commandments serve as the foundation of the entire Law. Perhaps we should say that the remaining laws in the Torah explicate the Ten Commandments, demonstrating how one ought to fulfill them in particular situations. In fact, some scholars believe that the entire law code of Deuteronomy (chs. 12–26) is structured according to the Ten Commandments.[3] The only part of the Law kept inside the ark of the covenant is the two tablets with the Ten Commandments.[4]

The title "Ten Commandments" comes, as we have seen, from the Bible itself, which three times uses the phrase (Exod 34:28; Deut 4:13; 10:4). But actually the word for "commandment" does not appear in these verses, which more literally speak of the "ten words," or, perhaps, the "ten statements," which explains the other common title for these laws, the "Decalogue," a Greek word meaning "ten words."

These passages reveal that we are supposed to find specifically ten statements or commandments in Exodus 20:1–17 and Deuteronomy 5:6–21. They tell us the number, but they do not tell us how to arrive at the number, so it may (or may not) be surprising that people have not always agreed on how to divide the Ten Commandments. Jews, Roman Catholics, and different Protestant groups have varied slightly in their arrangements of these commandments.

Readers of this lesson are probably most familiar with the following arrangement.

Commandment / Exodus 20:1–17
[1]Then God spoke all these words:

PROLOGUE

²I am the LORD your God, who brought you out of the land of Egypt, out of the house of slavery.

1. ³You shall have no other gods before me.
2. ⁴You shall not make for yourself an idol, or any likeness of what is in heaven above or on the earth beneath or in the water under the earth. ⁵You shall not worship them or serve them; for I, the LORD your God, am a jealous God, visiting the iniquity of the fathers on the children, on the third and the fourth generations of those who hate me, ⁶but showing lovingkindness to thousands, to those who love me and keep my commandments.
3. ⁷You shall not take the name of the LORD your God in vain, for the LORD will not leave him unpunished who takes his name in vain.
4. ⁸Remember the sabbath day, to keep it holy. ⁹Six days you shall labor and do all your work, ¹⁰but the seventh day is a sabbath of the LORD your God; in it you shall not do any work, you or your son or your daughter, your male or your female servant or your cattle or your sojourner who stays with you. ¹¹For in six days the LORD made the heavens and the earth, the sea and all that is

in them, and rested on the seventh day; therefore the LORD blessed the sabbath day and made it holy.

5. ¹²Honor your father and your mother, that your days may be prolonged in the land which the LORD your God gives you.
6. ¹³You shall not murder.
7. ¹⁴You shall not commit adultery.
8. ¹⁵You shall not steal.
9. ¹⁶You shall not bear false witness against your neighbor.
10. ¹⁷You shall not covet your neighbor's house; you shall not covet your neighbor's wife or his male servant or his female servant or his ox or his donkey or anything that belongs to your neighbor.

Jewish tradition has usually considered the Prologue to be the first "word" of the Ten Words, counting what is labeled above as commandments 1 and 2 together as the second "word."[5] But Jewish tradition is not uniform. One of the earliest Jewish orders that we can determine is found in the work of the first-century historian Josephus, who arranges the commandments precisely as in the list above.[6] On the other hand, the Samaritans, like the dominant Jewish tradition, combine commandments 1 and 2, thus making room within the Ten Commandments for an additional command found only in the Samaritan

Pentateuch, enjoining worship on Mt. Gerizim, the holy site of Samaritans.

There are also various Christian traditions regarding the grouping of these "words." The arrangement above finds expression in John Calvin's *Institutes of the Christian Religion* (2.8) from the sixteenth century. Calvin's older contemporary, Martin Luther, combined commandments 1 and 2, and so he divided the tenth commandment into two, calling the prohibition against coveting a neighbor's house the ninth commandment and the prohibition against coveting other assets of a neighbor the tenth commandment.[7] Similarly, the Catholic Church interprets commandments 1 and 2 as a single command, dividing the tenth commandment into two so that it partly addresses sexual lust and it partly addresses other ungodly desires.[8]

This survey of different arrangements for the Ten Commandments shows that very often the prohibition against worshiping other gods and the prohibition against making idols have been treated as a single "word." This combination certainly makes sense, but another venerable tradition separates these two prohibitions, which is the practice followed in this study.

Application

Jesus thought the whole Old Testament boiled down to how we treat people: "Do unto others as you would have them do unto you, for this is the Law and the Prophets" (Matt 7:12). He wanted his followers to understand that the religious revolution he came to inaugurate was in fundamental agreement with this Old Testament ethic. Surely there is no need here to demonstrate that Jesus considered proper behavior toward others to be the very essence of true religion. Sometimes he labels such behavior toward others "justice" or "mercy" (23:23), often he calls it "love." As it turns out, "love" is another way of summarizing the Law and the Prophets: "Love the Lord your God with all your heart, with all your soul, and with all your mind. This is the greatest and most important command. The second is like it: Love your neighbor as yourself. All the Law and the Prophets depend on these two commands" (22:37–40).

Whereas the Golden Rule is articulated entirely in terms of a person's treatment of other people, in the exposition of the two greatest commands, a person's love for neighbor is explicitly given second place behind that person's love for God. There is no inconsistency here, once we recognize that in the Bible our treatment of people serves as a concrete expression of our regard for God (1 John 3:17; 4:20). Leviticus 19, the passage from which Jesus draws his second greatest command (see v. 18), routinely punctuates its ethical exhortations with the declaration, "I am the LORD" (15x in the chapter). For instance:

> When you reap the harvest of your land, you are not to reap to the very edge of your field or gather the gleanings of your harvest. Do not strip your vineyard bare or gather its fallen grapes. Leave them for the poor and the resident alien; I am the LORD your God. (Lev 19:9–10)

Or, later:

> Do not oppress your neighbor or rob him. The wages due a hired worker must not remain with you until morning. Do not curse the deaf or put a stumbling block in front of the blind, but you are to fear your God; I am the LORD. (vv. 13–14)

Or, again:

> Do not harbor hatred against your brother. Rebuke your neighbor directly, and you will not incur guilt because of him. Do not take revenge or bear a grudge against members of your community, but love your neighbor as yourself; I am the LORD. (vv. 17–18)

According to Leviticus 19, a person's acknowledgment of the Lord's position as God entails certain behaviors toward other people, particularly behaviors like justice and mercy and love. So, there is no diminishment of the importance of the greatest command when some New Testament writers magnify love of neighbor as itself the fulfillment of the entire Law (cf. Rom 13:8–10; Gal 5:14; Jas 2:8). Love of neighbor and love of God go hand-in-hand.

And this is what the Ten Commandments also summarize. First we are to love God, demonstrating this love by denying our allegiance to any other god, shunning idolatry, properly using God's name, and setting aside time to worship him and contemplate his mighty deeds. Second, we should love our neighbor, especially by avoiding harming them in any way, whether through murder, adultery, stealing, or lying, even desiring their belongings. The transitional commandment about honoring parents fits both categories, in that it is an action directed to some very important neighbors who, in a sense, represent to us God's own authority.

Conclusion

God first reveals his ethical demands to Israel through the Ten Commandments, which serve as the first and foundational summary of God's covenant with his people. These commandments guided the ethical reflections of Jesus (Mark 7:10), Paul (Rom 13:8–10; Eph 6:1–4), and James (2:8–13). We can also use them to help us reflect on the ways we need to show our love for God and our love for our neighbors.

Discussion

1. What value do the Ten Commandments have for Christians today?
2. How are the prohibitions against other gods and against idolatry related, and how are they distinct?
3. What is the relationship between love for God and love for neighbor?
4. Do the Ten Commandments serve as a good summary or encapsulation of God's requirements for humanity?

Endnotes

1. See the Babylonian Talmud, tractate Makkot, 23b–24a.

2. On God's writing the Ten Commandments, see Exod 34:1; Deut 5:22; 9:10; 10:2; cf. Exod 34:28.

3. See Georg Braulik, "The Sequence of the Laws in Deuteronomy 12–26 and in the Decalogue," in *A Song of Power and the Power of Song: Essays on the Book of Deuteronomy*, ed. Duane L. Christensen (Winona Lake, IN: Eisenbrauns, 1993), 313–35.

4. Deut 10:5; cf. Exod 25:16, 21; 1 Kings 8:9; Heb 9:4.

5. See the Jerusalem Talmud, tractate Berakhot 1.4 in the edition of Tzvee Zahavy, trans., *The Talmud of the Land of Israel: A Preliminary Translation and Explanation*,

vol. 1: Berakhot (Chicago: University of Chicago Press, 1989), 42–44.

6. Josephus, *Antiquities of the Jews* 3.90–92. See also Philo, *On the Decalogue* 51, who presents the same basic arrangement but inverts the adultery and murder commands. This divergent order for the sixth and seventh commandments reflects a confusing picture in the manuscript history of the Septuagint, which probably originally had the order adultery/stealing/murder in Exodus and adultery/murder/stealing in Deuteronomy. For other orders for these commandments, see Jer 7:9; Hos 4:2; Matt 19:18 // Mark 10:19 // Luke 18:20; Rom 13:9.

7. See Luther's *Small Catechism*, available online: http://bookofconcord.org/smallcatechism.php#tencommandments.

8. See the *Catechism of the Catholic Church* 2.3, available online:

http://www.vatican.va/archive/ENG0015/_INDEX.HTM

2. THE CHRISTIAN AND OLD TESTAMENT LAW
NATHAN DAILY

Exodus 19:3–6

One Main Thing

Old Testament law is not simply a list of rules, but rather it reveals—in concert with the story of God—the gracious character of God and incites God's people toward examining priorities in hope of displaying a life of gratitude for God's gifts.

Introduction

Old Testament law consistently retains the status of one of the most difficult and underappreciated portions of Scripture for the Christian.

Readers are often more likely to turn toward the remainder of the Old Testament when contemplating

God, discussing faith, and reflecting upon the practice of Christian life.

- The explorations upon the meaning of a life filled with happiness and contentment as well as with suffering and death in wisdom literature like Proverbs, Job, and Ecclesiastes present readers with a posture for speech and action toward world and God even when God appears absent from the realities of the moment.
- The interplay between the stories of the past and the defense of God's goodness present in narrative books like Joshua, Judges, Samuel, and Kings offers readers an opportunity to reflect upon promise and covenant as guiding momentum within any crisis of the present.
- The hope for a future where God is king and divine presence is abundantly clear among a holy people in prophetic books like Isaiah, Ezekiel, and Zephaniah encourages readers to look for God's presence in the present even when anticipating the clarity of the future.
- The prayers of lament and praise addressing a powerful God of justice in poetic books like Psalms and Lamentations provide readers who undergo a loss for

> words when addressing the divine with the traditional language of the community of faith—a language that in candidness does not skirt sincerity or fear honesty, a language that assumes God is righteous, capable of action, and is even willing to hear human thoughts whether it be a time of anxiety, doubt, praise, or thanksgiving.

But for many believers, Old Testament law is an entirely different matter.

Going Deeper

Two questions can provide impetus for beginning to consider how Old Testament law might inform Christian practice: (1) Why do Christians sometimes avoid reading Old Testament law? and (2) What exactly is Old Testament law? The first question addresses common assumptions about Old Testament law and the second reframes expectations through observing the biblical presentation of law.

Confusion over how to read Old Testament law as Christian Scripture arises from a number of angles and might tempt readers to ignore rather than engage the books that contain law.

The material is simply difficult. Not only are the customs recounted in biblical law ancient and unfamiliar to modern Christian readers, the sacrifices that

The Christian and Old Testament Law

are a central aspect of the text are difficult to visualize for those who have never seen or participated in such a ritual. Nevertheless, the New Testament, particularly the book of Hebrews, demands engagement with the sacrificial system within Old Testament law for a proper understanding of an event of utmost importance to the Christian faith, the nature and ongoing significance of the death of Jesus Christ.[1]

2. Some readers uncritically view the ritualistic nature of law as negative. An aversion to ritual (sacrifices, ceremonies, holy days, laws) causes many to speak derogatorily about Old Testament law as old, boring, joyless, and, even worse, absent of heart or theologically empty—in spite of many biblical statements to the contrary.[2] In fact, we could argue ritual is the opposite of boring and heartless insofar as rituals are the repeated expressions of what move us the most (e.g., the Lord's Supper).

3. Several New Testament texts expound upon the obsolete nature of the ceremonial and sacrificial laws of Israel for Gentile Christians.[3] Even as these texts, written in a variety of polemical contexts, limit the use of Old Testament law for Christian practice, the very same texts appeal to Old Testament law to make their argument.[4] Thus, Christian readers do not ignore the law but hold together the limitations stated in the New Testament with the New Testament claim that *all* Scripture is the word of God and beneficial for theological reflection—"for teaching, for

reproof, for correction, and for training in righteousness."[5]

Since readers often get lost in the details of various laws, an initial step toward building an appreciation for reading Old Testament law as Scripture comes from defining the term "law" and recognizing how the Bible itself presents law. Christians traditionally label the first five books of the Bible as the books of Law. The Hebrew term *torah*, often translated as "law," is actually a broader term that means "teaching" or "instruction." These five books do contain many laws: the laws at Sinai,[6] the laws in the Wilderness,[7] and the laws presented by Moses to the generation entering the land.[8] Since the Torah, the first five books of the Bible, also contains narrative and poetry in addition to commandments, the terms "teaching" and "instruction" as translations of *torah* are helpful in that they point not only to the specific laws found within these books but also to the didactic nature of the narratives and poems of Genesis, Exodus, Leviticus, Numbers, and Deuteronomy.

This point is very important for understanding the character of the material. The Torah presents itself as story, and readers must not approach specific laws in isolation but as components of the Torah story. The specific laws receive meaning from the story that encapsulates them and the character of the God depicted within that story. The story of a God who speaks the cosmos into existence.[9] The story of a God who offers promise toward a family who will be a blessing for all families of the earth.[10] The story of a God who delivers from bondage and hopelessness.[11] The story of a God who appears, instructs, and is a holy presence among a people.[12] The story of a God who emphasizes love, relationship, and covenant for ongoing generations.[13] The story of a God who gives law because law promotes life and purpose for God's people[14] and reveals the character of the God who dwells among them.[15]

Application

Reading Old Testament law within the story of God provides a variety of avenues for theological reflection. Of many possibilities, three examples may serve as a starting point:

Salvation and the Story of Exodus: Exodus 19:3–6 grounds Old Testament law within the story of a gracious God who rescues and commissions a unique people for an expansive mission. Before God gives law, God rescues Israel and labels them a special people. When Israel arrives at Sinai, God's first statement recounts the Exodus from Egypt as an act of grace in response to desperate need.[16] Similarly, the Ten Commandments begin with a reminder of past salvation.[17] God's initial act of rescuing Israel is foundational for understanding the law at Sinai—grace precedes law. The story contextualizes the law in such a way that Israel's obedience is responsive thanksgiving to a gracious gift of salvation from the bondage of Egypt.[18] Further, adherence to the law is a purposeful response by this special people to contribute toward God's mission, the realization by all that the whole earth belongs to God.[19] The exchange between divine initiative and human response modeled in the Torah story remains a distinctive feature of the story of God as 1 Peter 2:9 shapes Christian identity and mission through allusion to Exodus 19:3–6—"But you are a chosen race, a royal priesthood, a holy nation, God's own people, in order that you may proclaim the mighty acts of him who called you out of darkness into his marvelous light"—or as 1 John plainly and profoundly affirms—"We love because he first loved us" (4:18).

Holiness and the Story of Leviticus: The Torah places Old Testament law within the story of a holy God whose presence impacts all spheres of life. Following the episode with the golden calf, uncertainty surrounds God's ongoing relationship with the people as they are in danger of losing access to the presence of God.[20] Once Moses intercedes for the people, the book of Exodus ends dramatically with the holy God inhabiting the tabernacle to dwell in the midst of Israel.[21] Throughout the following story, inattentiveness to the holiness of God as expressed in the Wilderness Wanderings is dangerous and may result in disaster.[22] Conversely, attention to God's holiness, as envisioned in Leviticus through sacrifice, purity, and order, results in a community that may be, just as the deity is, holy themselves.[23] In the Bible, holiness amounts to that which makes God "different" or "other" from all else (i.e., holy is ultimately "what God is"). Thus, the people of God derive a distinct (= holy) status from association with the presence of God. Following the injunction to be holy in Leviticus 19:2, the laws in 19:3–37 seemingly focus on almost every aspect of life: family relationships, idolatry, worship, compassion toward people with disabilities, fairness, charity, justice, and honesty. The list of such a wide variety of ethical commands interspersed regularly with the phrase "I am the LORD"[24] encourages those who are "to be holy" to recognize adherence to the commands in 19:3–37 as a mode for reflecting the holy character of God. Thus, when read with the Torah story's focus upon the presence of God, the laws enjoin practical behaviors that manifest mission—exhibiting Israel's identity as holy like the God they serve. As the holy God continually offers avenue for divine presence in the life of the believer,[25] Old Testament law challenges believers to imagine current ethical circumstances in light of ancient Israel's holiness guidelines in an attempt to conform action to the character of the divine one, that is, in the words of 1 Peter — "as he who called you is holy, be holy yourselves in all your conduct; for it is written, 'You shall be holy, for I am holy'" (1:15–16).

Love and the Story of Deuteronomy: Too often overlooked, the dynamic influence of love initiates and sustains relationship for generations in Old Testament law. God's love for Israel's ancestors provides a foundational ingredient for Israel's rescue from Egypt and the subsequent gift of law.[26] Israel's reciprocation of love toward God is among the base requirements within the covenantal relationship.[27] Maintenance of the relationship is exhibited vertically through ongoing love of and from God[28] as well as horizontally toward the orphan, widow, and stranger.[29] As God's love for Israel goes back to the time of Abraham and Sarah, love is also an ongoing expectation for coming generations of God's people.[30] The Torah story does not present law as a mechanism for earning God's favor.[31] Instead, God's love for Israel predates law, and Israel's love for God is an avenue leading toward obedience to the entirety of the commandments.[32] The language of love in the Torah accentuates the relational and personalized dimension of Old Testament law. The New Testament retains the sense of the connection between love and action—"For the love of God is this, that we obey his commandments. And his commandments are not burdensome."[33] Love from God,[34] love for God,[35] and love of neighbor[36] remain at the core of the language of faith with their clarity and simplicity and, paradoxically, their demanding profundity when contemplating the multitude of options for practice each day (1 John 4:12, 20–21).

Conclusion

Christians who want to read and understand Old Testament law are not attempting to become ancient Israelites or follow stipulations meant for another time and place. Rather, a goal for Christians who approach the Torah as Scripture (2 Tim 3:16) is to better understand the character of God and humanity's relationship to that God. Though many specific laws will remain difficult to understand, the hope is to read the Torah, both story and command together, in such a way that the prevalent themes of presence, holiness, justice, giving, family, leadership, sin, righteousness, love, wisdom, and many others emerge in all their complexity as stimuli for introspection and practice in Christian life.

Discussion

1. Why do many Christians find Old Testament law more difficult to read than other parts of the Old Testament?
2. Define the word "ritual." What are some rituals in your personal life? In your religious life? Why do you repeat these actions? How do they add meaning and joy to your life?
3. Choose one or more of the following verses

and discuss how a knowledge of Old Testament law is helpful for understanding the Christian faith: Heb 7–10; Matt 20:28; John 19:36; Acts 8:32–35; Rom 8:3, 32; 1 Cor 5:7; 2 Cor 5:21; 1 Pet 2:22; 1 John 1:7; 2:2.
4. What is "all Scripture" in 2 Tim 3:16? What is all Scripture "for" according to this verse?
5. What is the meaning of the Hebrew word *torah*? Why is it important to recognize Old Testament law occurs within the context of a story?
6. Consider the application themes (grace before command, divine presence and holiness, love for generations). How does the emphasis on each theme in the Old Testament help us think about who God is, our relationship to God, and our own mission within the story of God? How are or how could these themes be visible in your own life?

Endnotes

1. Heb 7–10; Matt 20:28; John 19:36; Acts 8:32–35; Rom 8:3, 32; 1 Cor 5:7; 2 Cor 5:21; 1 Pet 2:22; 1 John 1:7; 2:2.

2. Deut 4:1; 10:10–15; Ps 1:1–2; 119:1–176; Rom 7:12–14; 1 Tim 1:8.

3. Mk 7; Rom 7:1–7; 2 Cor 3; Gal 3–4; Heb 7–10; cf. Titus 3:9.

4. Esp. Gal 3–4 and Heb 7–10.
5. 2 Tim 3:16; cf. Rom 7:12–14; 1 Tim 1:8.
6. Exod 19:1–Num 10:10.
7. Num 10:11–36:13.
8. Deut 4:44–28.
9. Gen 1:1–11:26.
10. Gen 11:27–50:26.
11. Exod 1:1–18:27.
12. Exod 19:1–Num 36:13.
13. Deut 1:1–34:12
14. Exod 19:4–6; Deut 4:1–8; 5:33; 32:46–47.
15. Exod 34:4–7; 40:33b–38; Lev 19:2, 18, 34; Deut 10:17–18.
16. Cf. Exod 2:23; 3:7–9.
17. Exod 20:2.
18. Deut 26:4–11.
19. Exod 19:5–6; cf. Deut 26:16–19; Exod 6:7; 14:18; 16:6; Isa 49:6.
20. Exod 33:12–23; cf. 29:42–46.
21. Exod 40:34–38.
22. Exod 16–18; 32–34; Num 10–25.
23. Lev 11:45; 19:2.
24. Lev 19:3, 10, 12, etc.
25. John 1:14; 1 Cor 3:16–17.
26. Deut 4:37; 7:7–9; 23:5.
27. Deut 10:12; 11:1, 13; 19:9.
28. Deut 6:5; 7:13; 10:18.
29. Deut 10:18–19; cf. 29:17.
30. Deut 7:9, 13; 30:6.

31. Deut 9:4.
32. Deut 30:11–16; cf. 19:9; 11:13.
33. 1 John 5:3; cf. Deut 30:11, 16.
34. Rom 5:8; 8:28; Gal 2:20; Eph 2:4; 1 John 4:10–11.
35. 1 Cor 2:9; 8:3; 1 John 5:2–3.
36. Rom 13:8, 10; Gal 5:14; Jas 2:8; 1 Thess 4:9.

3. I AM THE LORD YOUR GOD
THE PROLOGUE TO THE TEN COMMANDMENTS

JEREMY BARRIER

Exodus 20:1–2

One Main Thing

God makes a public declaration to his people that he is the LORD. The LORD's dominion means both freedom from any suppressing powers of this earth and complete *compliance* to his moral structuring of the cosmos.

Introduction

"Dear members of the city council …." That is how I began my 90-second speech, as I felt a small bead of sweat running down my temple and onto my cheek. I was nervous, excited, and feeling very indecisive on what words would be my next words. I was addressing the city council in my hometown for the first time concerning a matter that was dear to my heart, and the six councilmen who were looking down on me with cold, hard—yet gentle—faces weren't helping calm the butterflies in my stomach. Neither were the one hundred fellow citizens of Florence helping either as they were patiently waiting for their turn to speak.

If you had the chance to address your home congregation, community, or city and make some kind of statement concerning who you are and what you expect of others, what would you say? While you might not desire this opportunity, you can imagine that it would be difficult to put your thoughts into words.

We see a similar situation in Exodus 20, a text that begins with a typical ancient Near Eastern formal announcement by a royal who is about to express his sovereignty and make clear his identity to Moses and the children of Israel. This passage is important and just might be the most important declaration by God within the five books of Moses.

The Ten Commandments are located in the center of a 40-chapter book, so that they form the fulcrum and centerpiece of the book of Exodus. Here we encounter the Jewish idea of completion (i.e., the number 10), yet we can tell that each command clearly represents a typical, archaic, and short statement referring to either God or God's requirement. Most telling are commandments 6, 7, and 8, which (in Hebrew, at least) each constitute only two words. These commandments—short, terse statements—are well-

I Am the Lord Your God

suited to being written on stone, then duplicated and sent throughout the tribes of Israel. To introduce this text, Exodus 20:1–2 tells us that, "God *spoke* all these words" (emphasis added). The very God who *spoke* the earth into existence in Genesis speaks again. Just as God spoke and brought order to the natural world, so also now God speaks and brings order to the social and moral aspect of the universe—a perfect declaration by God. Following the royal declaration and announcement that the LORD's divine presence is "in the house" in Exodus 20:1–2, what follows will truly be a profound introduction to the God who speaks and provides guidance to his people.

Going Deeper

Several elements of this text help us understand our God. First, God *speaks* to Israel. Even when God is choosing to organize and define the moral order of the cosmos, he still makes the decision to involve humans in the process! At every stage, God is involving humanity in the unfolding of his designs.

A further detail worth mentioning has to do with the expression "ten commandments." As we saw in the previous lesson, verses like Exodus 34:28 literally talk not about commandments but words or, perhaps even, ideas. Once we realize that these are ten ideas, words, matters, or concepts that the LORD presents to Israel, then we, as readers, begin to understand that these statements are as much about Israel perceiving the nature of God as they were about Israel grasping their responsibilities to God.

Last, and probably most important to understanding this passage, is the last line, "I am the LORD your God who brought you out of the land of Egypt, out of the house of slaves." This line, as noted, is a royal announcement about who will address the hearers. Within the framework of Exodus, this passage probably has a fitting partner in Exodus 3:3–16. In this previous chapter, God introduces himself to Moses at the burning bush as "I AM" and "The LORD, the God of your ancestors, the God of Abraham, the God of Isaac, and the God of Jacob, has sent me to you." Further, he tells Moses to go to "the land of Egypt" (also known in Exodus 20 as the "house of slaves") and tell Pharaoh and all of Egypt that the LORD has come to deliver Israel. Clearly, by the time the narrative arrives at Exodus 20, God's declaration of himself has expanded. In both cases, God identifies himself based on his relationship to humanity. The LORD is first a God who delivers a family. Then, he is a God of deliverance, a God who overthrows nations, a God who overtakes the oppressor, lifts up those who have been suppressed unjustly, and protects those who have no protector. This is the God who is going to give his commandments and define his way of life to Israel.

Application

God has been speaking to humanity since the beginning of time. Are you listening? Too many people live their lives and only too late in life do they realize that the same God who gave shape and order to the cosmos desires to give shape and order to our individual lives, our family, and our community. Are you listening for the voice of God?

Second, these commandments should cause us to not only ask, "What does God require of me?" but to also ask, "Who is this God?" These words draw us out of ourselves and encourage us to explore God and the nature of God—a daunting, yet exhilarating experience.

Third, when we begin to realize that we have come to the foot of Mt. Sinai to experience God, we just might comprehend that the first words by God tell us his name and that he comes in peace. God wants it to be clear that he has not come to Israel to bring harm or oppression, but—quite the contrary—to bring liberation. God is the God of freedom. While the new covenant that God has extended to us today may be altered from the one at Sinai, the nature of God's offering of freedom has not. Knowing these three facets should offer you solace, peace, and comfort as you read the remainder of the commandments in Exodus 20.

Conclusion

The story of Israel is amazing. This story tells us of a God who singled out a person and a people. This story gives us the liberation of the suppressed Israel to the domineering Egyptians. The overthrow of Egypt comes in the early chapters of Exodus, then the ten plagues, and finally the casting down of the oppressor into the Red Sea. What an exciting story of people who can overcome in the face of such difficult odds. After these monumental and liberating events, the culmination of it all is the giving of the Ten Commandments and the announcement to Israel, that this God, the LORD, is the one who made it all possible. This is the God who is worthy to be listened to, and worthy to be served. It is no wonder that so many social movements across time and space have used such a powerful story to lift people up and give hope to the masses. In the same way that so many in the past have cried out for deliverance, maybe you also, in your moments of despair will have the hope and courage to hear the voice of the LORD God when he speaks to you and says, "I am the LORD your God who delivers you."

Discussion

1. How does God initially deliver "these

I Am the Lord Your God

words," the Ten Commandments, to Israel? Is the form of delivery important?

2. What is the name of God in this passage? How does God identify himself?
3. In Exodus 20, God is now more than the "God of Abraham, Isaac, and Jacob," but now the God who "brought you out of the land of Egypt." What does this tell you about God's power and sovereignty?
4. If God had dominion even over the greatest of nations on the earth, namely Egypt, doesn't this imply that God can have dominion in your life, if you desire it?

4. NO OTHER GODS
W. KIRK BROTHERS

Exodus 20:3

One Main Thing

The Ten Commandments are the ten wedding vows for God's marriage with Israel. At the heart of the laws is a relationship.

Introduction

I refer to the events of Exodus 19–20 as "The Marriage on the Mountain." The section we refer to as "The Ten Commandments" is given various labels in Scripture:

1. "The Ten Commandments" (Exod 34:28)
2. "The words of the covenant" (Deut 34:28)
3. "The tables of the covenant" (Deut 9:9)

4. "The covenant" (Deut 4:13)
5. "The two tables" (Deut 9:10–17)
6. "The testimony" (Exod 16:34; 25:16)
7. "The tablets of the testimony" (Exod 31:18)
8. "The commandments" (Matt 19:17)

I prefer to refer to them as "The Ten Vows." I understand that this phrase is not found in Scripture, yet it does illustrate the significance of these sayings. If we can see these events as a wedding proposal and a wedding ceremony, then it can not only transform how we understand these sayings, it can transform how we view all of Scripture. This lesson focuses on the first commandment in terms of a covenant relationship, a marriage ceremony.

Going Deeper

The Proposal

Before there can be a wedding, there has to be a proposal and the acceptance of that proposal. Exodus 19 contains the proposal from God and its acceptance. Moses delivers the proposal on behalf of the Creator. In fact, Exodus 19–34 finds Moses traveling up and down the mountain numerous times carrying messages to and from God.

- Trip 1: God offers covenant to Moses (19:3–7)

- Trip 2: Moses reports & the people accept (19:8–15)
- Trip 3: God tells Moses how to prepare (19:20–25)
- Trip 4: God gives Law in greater detail (20:1–32:33)
- Trip 5: God meets with Israelite leaders (24:9–11)
- Trip 6: God gives tabernacle guidance (24:12–31:18)
- Trip 7: Moses receives Law second time (34)

The proposal itself can be found in Exodus 19:4–6:

> You yourselves have seen what I did to the Egyptians, and *how* I bore you on eagles' wings, and brought you to Myself. Now then, if you will indeed obey My voice and keep My covenant, then you shall be My own possession among all the peoples, for all the earth is Mine; and you shall be to Me a kingdom of priests and a holy nation.

God begins by reminding them of how much he loves them. He loved them enough to deliver them from the hands of the Egyptians. He wants them to be his own people. He is offering a covenant relationship to them. He also tells them that this is a proposal with a purpose. They are to be a "kingdom of priests" (19:6). Priests function as mediators between God and human beings. Many falsely assume that the Father chose Israel because he did not care about the rest of humanity. He actually chose them as a kingdom of priests who were to help the rest of the world to know about him. Israel, by and large, forgot this purpose. Moses delivered the proposal to the elders of Israel and they said, "Yes": "All that the Lord has spoken we will do!" (Exod 19:8).

The Ceremony

God arrives for the wedding ceremony in all his regal splendor. The mountain explodes in fire and smoke from his presence (Exod 19:16-19). Fire is regularly associated with the presence of God in Scripture:

- Burning Bush (Exodus 3)
- Fiery Pillar (Exodus 13)
- Mount Sinai (Exodus 24)
- Tongues of Fire (Acts 2)

It is important for Israel to know with whom they are entering a relationship. This is the creator of all that is. To enter into a covenant with him is not a trivial thing. God also reminds them that he cares about them: "I am the Lord your God, who brought you out of the land of Egypt, out of the house of slavery" (Exod 20:2). It is this dual understanding of God's greatness and love that is going to be important as foundations for their relationship together.

Wedding ceremonies typically feature the exchanging of vows. An example might be as follows:

> Do you, _____, take this _____ to be Your wedded _____, to live together after God's ordinances in the holy state of matrimony? To love, comfort, cherish, honor and keep in sickness and in health, in prosperity and adversity; and, forsaking all others, keep yourself only for _____, as long as you both shall live?

The vows describe the level of commitment the two are making to each other. Their love will continue in sickness and health and in prosperity and adversity.

The commandments found in Exodus 20:3 and following are the vows for the wedding ceremony between God and Israel. These vows flow out of the two great commands: 1) Love God and 2) Love your neighbor (Matt 22:37–40). Love for your neighbor can be found in vows 5–10 and love for God can be found in vows 1–4. For a marriage to last, a couple must share some core values that they hold in common. If one believes that it is a good idea to rob banks and kill people and the other does not, it is going to be hard for their marriage to survive.

Vows 5–10 highlight the common values God and Israel are to share: respect for others, faithfulness, honesty, etc. Couples in a marriage relationship should also be committed and faithful to each other. That is what commandments/vows 1–4 are about. They are nothing more than the reasonable expectations of someone making a lifetime commitment to the one he or she loves.

God says, "You shall have no other gods before me" (Exod 20:3). This is no different from a husband expecting his spouse to "keep yourself only for him, as long as you both shall live." In fact, you might put the first four commandments in modern terms as follows:

- No other gods: Don't sleep with another man
- No images: No pictures of old boyfriends in your wallet
- Name in vain: Do not dishonor my name
- Sabbath: Make time for me in your weekly schedule

God has been and will be faithful to Israel. He wants them to be faithful to him. Idolatry was a way of life in the ancient world. God consistently referred to worship of false gods as adultery in Scripture.

A tremendous example of this is found in the book of Hosea. Hosea was to marry a prostitute because this prostitute became a living illustration of Judah's unfaithfulness to God (Hos 1:2). They were told to name their second child, "Lo-ammi, for you are not my people and I am not your God" (1:8). Lo-ammi means "not my people." Contrast this with God's statement in Exodus 19:5, "Now then, if you will indeed obey my voice and keep my covenant, then you shall be *my own possession among all the peoples*, for all the earth is mine" (emphasis mine). They had failed to keep their wedding vows. God goes on to declare, "Contend with your mother, contend, for she is not my wife, and I am not her husband; and let her put away her harlotry from her face and her adultery from between her breasts" (Hos 2:2). God does not take unfaithfulness to him lightly.

When one reads through the books of 1 and 2 Kings, one finds that the kings were not evaluated so much on their military or economic prowess as their faithfulness to God. An example of this can be found in 1 Kings 11:1–8. Solomon took many wives and concubines "who turned his heart aside after other gods; and his heart was not wholly devoted to the Lord, as the heart of his father David had been" (11:4). King David had his issues, but one thing you could say about him is that he was a one-God man. He never worshiped any idols. That can be said of very few of the kings of Israel and Judah. Most of these kings forgot the commitment to have no other gods that their nation made in the original wedding ceremony with God. God is regularly described as a jealous God (Exod 20:5; 34:14; Deut 4:24; 5:9; etc.). He wants Israel all to himself. That is what any bride or groom would want from his or her spouse.

Application

The first thing we must remember is that God uses the same language of the church that he used of ancient Israel. Consider Peter's words:

> But you are a chosen race, a royal priesthood, a holy nation, a people for *God's* own possession, so that you may proclaim the excellencies of Him who has called you out of darkness into His marvelous light; for you once were not a people, but now you are the people of God; you had not received mercy, but now you have received mercy. (1 Peter 2:9–10)

We too are "a people of God's possession." We are his people and should be faithful to him. Are we? We are also "a royal priesthood." We are his representatives in the world to help the world know about him. Are we living up to this responsibility?

The second thing that can be helpful in light of this passage is to see the commands in Scripture in terms of a relationship. The 600+ commands in Scripture are basically expansions and applications of the ten found in Exodus 20. The Ten are expansions of the two great commands (Matt 22:37–40) which are basically the expansion of the one great command: "You shall love the Lord your God with all your heart, and with all your soul, and with all your mind" (Matt 22:37). All of Scripture boils down to love for and faithfulness to the

God who loves us and is faithful to us. Understanding this can transform how we view commands in God's word and the very nature of our Christian lives.

Conclusion

I do not need a command to make me be faithful to my wife, Cindy. I love her with all my heart. I could not imagine being with anyone else. I would never want to do anything to violate her trust. It should be the same in our relationship with God. It is my prayer that this lesson will transform how we view Scripture. Commands are not just checklists for avoiding hell or to access heaven. They are the vows for our wedding ceremony with God. They represent the level of commitment to God and the values we share with him. They are just what you do when you are in love.

Discussion

1. Why do you think Israel was unfaithful to God (golden calf) even after seeing his greatness on the mountain?
2. How can viewing the Ten Commandments as wedding vows change us?
3. What are the implications of being a "royal priesthood" for evangelism?

4. What are some ways in which we are unfaithful to God?

5. NO IDOLS
ARVY DUPUY

Exodus 20:4–6

One Main Thing

Idolatry is a constant temptation for humans that always leads to disastrous results and distorts our view of God.

Introduction

Margaret Heffernan, in her book *Willful Blindness*, explores why we choose—sometimes consciously, but mostly not—to remain unseeing in situations where "we could know, and should know, but don't know because it makes us feel better not to know."[1] We might see something a certain way and never consider any other option.

Could this be the case with the second commandment of the Ten? We understand that commandment so well, we do not even have to give it a second thought. But it is the second thought that brings it into modern application. It is the second thought that will challenge us to open our eyes to our condition and possibly to our own denial of the truth within.

Going Deeper

What is the first thing that comes to your mind when you hear the world "idol"? An ancient carved image to which people bow down? Perhaps we make a connection with Hindus, Buddhists, or other modern-day idolaters praying at public temples to a variety of carved images. In Fiji, my wife and I befriended a sweet lady of the Hindu faith. She invited us to her home and proudly showed us her private shrine. There were several statues representing the gods that she and her family prayed to daily. That is the image that comes to my mind when I read these verses. I want to leave the meaning there with the idolaters, because it makes me comfortable. If I can leave it there, I feel secure—I definitely do not violate this edict from God.

If we dare to take a second look, we have to begin with the ideology behind the theology. What caused God to tell his people this? Was God threatened by a carved block of wood or a molded piece of clay?

Certainly not. Of course, he did not want Israel to be like the nations around them that ran after others gods while forgetting him. But if we could reason out the full intent of the command, we might be able to apply a broader definition, even one that confronts and warns us today.

The book of Judges shows us the outcome of willful blindness to this commandment, the application and non-application of this command. Judges 2:2–3 might lead us to ask how false gods can be a thorn and a snare. God knew that idols would cause Israel great harm. Idolatry goes far beyond just turning from God; it is about our well-being and success. Today we might worship money, a career, material possessions, making those things our sources of security, identity, happiness, and joy. An idol is anything that we add to God as a requirement for being happy and complete. When we make something into an idol it will eventually make us miserable because it has the capacity only to hurt us and rob us of joy. An idol cannot offer us forgiveness. If we make our children or grandchildren our idols, and they begin having problems, we are robbed of joy because what we worship has not lived up to our expectation. These things become a snare to us because idols enslave us. We must possess it to be happy; we cannot say "no" to it; we become addicted.

We see this pattern with Israel in the book of Judges. Every time Israel worshiped the idols of

No Idols

another nation, that nation ended up oppressing Israel. In Judges 10:6, the words used are "served" and "sold." Then in verse 11, seven nations oppressed Israel, which directly parallels the sevenfold idolatry of verse 6. Their idolatry led to slavery, and their slavery led to idolatry. One would think that if a nation were oppressing Israel, the Israelites would hate the gods of that nation. But Israel ends up serving the gods of the nations that conquered them, and that, in turn, just leads to greater enslavement.

Despite pain and anguish, the people of Israel continue to worship the same idols that have done nothing for them but brought them trouble. We do the same thing. We become blind to the warnings of God. We idolize the very things that bring us pain and disappoint. When we do this, we only magnify our pain and disappointment.

When God "sold" the Israelites because of their idolatry, he did not abandon them or nullify his promises to them. But he did stop protecting them in some ways. He let the things they had been serving actually begin to dominate and "own" them.

Application

Paul provides a fascinating parallel passage in Romans 1:24–25, where the word "lusts" appears—a word that, in Greek, means an overwhelming drive, an enslaving, uncontrollable desire. God "gives up" people, indicating that he allows the things we trust—that substitute for God in our lives—to become ruling powers over us. It is a punishment of "natural consequences." Idolatry and slavery go hand in hand. Idolatry leads to slavery, and slavery to idolatry.

Today our greatest danger is not that we will have no gods at all—that we will become atheists—but that we will have too many gods, allowing idols to have a part of our hearts where only God belongs.

Moreover, if we were to make an idol, something physically representing the true God, we would be exhibiting only part of God's character while concealing other parts. If you painted a picture of God, would it show him smiling and loving, or furious and majestic? An image cannot express the full range of God's glory; idolatry necessarily distorts our view of God.

When we begin to shape God so that he is manageable and controllable, we tend to omit the parts of his character that we do not like. Worshiping God with images reveals that a spirit within us that does not want to submit to God as he truly is, but that wants to pick and choose attributes in order to create a God who is agreeable to us.

This is why God commands us to submit to his revelation of himself. How do we violate this today? It is as simple as refusing to let God be himself in our lives. We filter out—consciously or unconsciously—

No Idols

things about God our hearts won't accept. We say, "I don't believe in a God like that! I like to think of God as ..."? That is worshiping God through the work of our own hands.

We can be guilty of this strategy both intellectually and psychologically. Most seriously, we intellectually reject part of the Scriptural revelation of God. We do this whenever we say, "I can no longer accept a God who does this, or who forbids that." When we use the term "no longer," we wrap ourselves in the mantle of progress. We are really saying, "Our culture's distaste for this idea means we must drop it! We must have a God who fits our culture's sensibilities." We reshape God to fit our society and hearts instead of letting God reshape our hearts and society.

We can also (psychologically) ignore or avoid aspects of revelation we don't like. God is very strong on forgiveness and grace, yet we may be very judgmental and unforgiving. We may know about passages on grace and mercy, but we have never really "heard" them—we have not really "seen" God for who he is. The bottom line and greatest dilemma is that it makes it impossible to have a truly personal relationship with God. In a genuine relationship, the other person can contradict us, upset us and then we have to wrestle with and work through those emotions to deeper intimacy. But when we simply ignore (intellectually or psychologically) the parts of God we don't like, it means we do not have a God who can ever contradict our deepest desires or say "no" to us. We never wrestle with him. He never makes demands on us.

In reality, the root of almost every personal problem is a refusal to let God be himself. It is a failure to accept and embrace God as he truly is.

Why does God forbid making images of him? For all these reasons and more, but the bottom line is this: he forbids because he has already given us an image of himself. Jesus Christ is the literal image of the invisible God (Col 1:16). He fulfills our need for a concrete way to see God's glory. Christ reveals to us God's perfect image.

Conclusion

Does the second commandment apply to me today? Absolutely, in ways we might not have ever considered but in ways that open eyes and with which receptive hearts will wrestle every day. Theologian Tim Keller says that the sin behind the sin is always idolatry. In the end, we all want a God that does not make demands on us.

Discussion

1. When you think of the word "idol," what is the first thing that comes to your mind?

2. What things or people determine your emotions?
3. How does worry derive from a distorted image of God?

Endnotes

1. Margaret Heffernan, *Willful Blindness: Why We Ignore the Obvious at Our Peril* (New York: Bloomsbury USA, 2011), 248.

6. THE NAME OF THE LORD
BILL BAGENTS

Exodus 20:7

One Main Thing

While respect for God's name offers tremendous blessing, the misuse of his name brings fearsome consequences.

Introduction

God's name holds tremendous importance throughout Scripture. It was noteworthy when "men began to call on the name of the Lord" (Gen 4:26). Scripture describes Abraham's worship as calling on the name of the Lord (Gen 12:8, 13:4, 16:13, 21:33). Moses identified the chosen nation as those who "are called by the name of the Lord" (Deut 28:10). As God's nation, God's people were to proclaim (Exod 33:19), minister in (Deut 18:5, 7), praise (Ps 7:17), call on (Ps 116:4; Joel 2:32), bless (Ps 113:2), remember (Ps 20:7), fear (Ps 102:15; Isa 59:19), trust (Isa 50:10; Zeph 3:12), walk in (Mic 4:5), and love (Isa 56:6) the name of the Lord.

Those truths offer tremendous background for our understanding of Exodus 20:7 as a powerful understatement. God's people do not take God's name in vain. Rather, we honor (Ps 66:2), revere (Mal 2:5), and reverence it (Ps 89:3).

The Bible notes the importance and blessing of knowing the name of the God whom we serve. It could be argued that the best question Moses asks God in Exodus 3 is, "... [When] they say to me, 'What is His name?' What shall I say to them?" God's answer is not a proper noun. Rather, he offers the dynamic and engaging, "I Am Who I Am." The name of God is more than Adonai, Yahweh, Elohim, Jehovah, or any word that humans might utter. The Lord and his name, in more ways than we know, stand beyond our comprehension. And yet by revelation, God's people know his name, his character, his will, and his love.

Going Deeper

In what ways could a person "take the name of the Lord your God in vain"?

We tend to think first of overt profanity, pairing

God's name with the vulgar and the crass. In addition to the passages cited above, Ephesians 4:29 and 5:4 forbid the very thought of using God's name as part of an expletive.

We also think of using God's name in frivolous ways, as a byword. The most common current example, "Oh my god!" is so common that it is seldom typed as in this sentence. People know OMG when they read it.

Vain use of God's name suggested by the context of Exodus 20 includes labeling as gods items or entities that are not (Exod 20:3). Things carved or molded are not God and must not be so labeled. God cannot be adequately or meaningfully represented by the work of human hands.

The Old Testament powerfully condemns taking God's name in vain by falsely claiming to speak in his name. Jeremiah 14:13–16 offers a chilling example. Prophets claimed to speak in his name, but the Lord says, "I have not sent them, commanded them, nor spoken to them; they prophesy to you a false vision …" And the consequences of their falsity are sword, famine, and destruction. It fits our focus passage so well, "You shall not take the name of the Lord your God in vain, for the Lord will not leave him unpunished who takes his name in vain." From Matthew 15:7–9, quoting Isaiah 20:13, we see those who draw near to God with their lips, but not with their hearts. They teach for commandments the doctrines of men, as if those commandments came from God. They take God's name in vain even as they offer him vain worship.

There is also a behavioral aspect of taking the Lord's name in vain. Titus 1:10–16 describes false Christians who teach false doctrine for personal profit. The passage concludes, "They profess to know God, but in works they deny Him, being abominable, disobedient, and disqualified for every good work." They falsely claim to speak in God's name and for God's glory, but their works, including their words, deny him.

Could one take God's name in vain in the sacred act of prayer? God does not violate his word or his character. Praying contrary to God's revelation is vain, presumptuous, and counter-productive (Jas 4:13–17; Matt 26:39, 42). Praying selfishly or pridefully cannot honor God's name (Luke 18:9–14; Jas 4:1–6). The same could be said of praying frivolously or faithlessly (Jas 1:5–8).

What of "the Lord will not leave him unpunished who takes his name in vain"?

This phrase stands as one of the classic examples of restraint and understatement within Scripture. It resonates with Galatians 6:7, "Do not be deceived; God is not mocked; for whatever a man sows, that he will also reap." It affirms Numbers 32:23, "... Be sure your sin will find you out." It supports Proverbs 13:15, "... But the way of the unfaithful is hard." Ultimately, it stands with Romans 11:22, affirming both the goodness and the severity of the Lord. Yet, we dare not affirm that God's punishment is limited to the eternal realm. Jeremiah uses fascinating language in describing the punishment of the false prophets who claim to speak in God's name and those who follow them, "… for I will pour their wickedness on them" (Jer 14:16). Their wickedness—the wickedness that they chose and practiced. Their wickedness earned their punishment.

Application

What implications does Exodus 20:7 hold for Christians today?

We know to avoid profanity, even that which does not directly blaspheme God. We also know not to use God's name in the more classic sense of the word "profane"—to use God's name in non-sacred, unworthy, or dishonorable ways. It is neither wise nor right to use God's name as a byword. We know it is unwise to use euphemisms that disrespect Deity. Out of respect for God, we avoid golly, gosh, gee, geez, Jesus H. Christ, and the like. In keeping with Matthew 7:1–6, we start by cleaning up our own speech as needed. It may be that we need help in this process of cleanup. We can ask others to pray for us, encourage us, and hold us accountable for the wise commitments we have made.

As parents, we teach our children to avoid language that demeans God. As friends and brethren, we kindly educate fellow Christians if they use such words. We do so within the spirit of Matthew 7:12, Galatians 6:1–2, Ephesians 4:15, and James 5:19–20. We do not assume that others know all that we know. We teach by word and example in humility and love.

We exercise great caution and respect when speaking of or for God. We refuse to elevate our opinions to the status of divine revelation (Matt 15:8–9). Out of respect for the Lord we remember and practice 1 Peter 4:11, "If anyone speaks, let him speak as the oracles of God." We refuse to add to or take from God's revelation (Rev 22:18–19).

Valuing Titus 1:16 and Matthew 7:21–23, we seek strong congruence between our words and our actions. Think of the football player who unleashes a streak of insult or profanity before turning to the camera to thank his Lord and Savior Jesus Christ for letting him have a great game. The praise rings hollow, even to the point of mockery. What a blessing when our lives speak of love and respect for God!

We choose to employ the wisdom of James 4:15, "If the Lord wills, we shall live and do this or that." We can regularly and appropriately say, "If the Lord wills …," acknowledging our faith in, awareness of, and submission to the Almighty.

And what happens if we find ourselves in the poor position of having used God's name in vain? We embrace the attitude of Job from Job 42:1–6. We affirm God's greatness, we admit our error, and we seek His forgiveness. We see that same attitude in Paul under very trying circumstances (Acts 23:1–5). What's wrong is wrong, even when we are under stress and pressure. When we find ourselves wrong before God, we change directions.

Conclusion

As Christians we continually seek ways to show increasing respect and adoration for God. He made us in his image (Gen 1:26–27). "In him we live and move and have our being" (Acts 17:28). He has extended and demonstrated his love for us in the most stunning of ways (John 3:16; Rom 5:8). We owe him everything.

We recognize and celebrate God's supremacy. We have given our lives to him. We never want to dishonor or disparage his name. We are blessed to esteem him above all. As we esteem and honor him, he draws us ever nearer to his heart.

Discussion

1. In what ways can taking the Lord's name in vain harm the person who does so?
2. Why might some be tempted to restrict "taking the Lord's name in vain" to overt profanity?
3. In what effective and encouraging ways

The Name of the Lord

have you heard others elevate and honor God's name?
4. What blessings will be reaped by the person who excels in honoring God's name?
5. What can we do to help one another excel in the grace of honoring God's name?

7. KEEPING THE SABBATH
C. WAYNE KILPATRICK

Exodus 20:8–11

One Main Thing

When we misunderstand the difference between the Sabbath and the first day of the week, we misunderstand the difference between the Old Testament and the New Testament.

Introduction

This collection of law transitions from the personal rights of God to the Sabbath, God's day of rest. The first three commandments are purely moral, while the fourth commandment is partly moral and partly positive. The idea that man's time should be divided between labor and time for the worship of God is moral. The division of the week following God's example in the creation is positive. The first three commandments are universally binding to man in relationship to his respecting God. The fourth is based on six days of work and the seventh as a day of rest. It was a perpetual obligation to Israel to remember the seventh day and its significance.

To hallow the Sabbath is to set it apart from any other day as a sacred day of rest. For "Six days thou shalt labor, and do all thy work" (Exod 20:9). Then you shall "Remember the Sabbath, to keep it holy" (Exod 20:8). The seventh day is for rest from work. The number seven has acquired a typical sacredness from its application to the Sabbath. It is the rest for God after six days of creation. Rest and dedication to God are the properties here assigned to the Sabbath. A reason is given for the observance of the fourth commandment. It refers to the original division of time into six days of work and a seventh day to rest (Gen 2:3). God not only rested from six days of creative labor, but blessed the Sabbath day and hallowed it (Exod 20:11).

This commandment raises a critical question for the New Testament church: how do Christians respond to the Sabbath day? Should we hallow it today? Are we wrong for not worshipping on Saturday, the Old Testament Jewish Sabbath Day? If the Sabbath is still bound upon the New Testament church, then we must observe it—not on Sunday but the seventh day (Saturday).

Going Deeper

Those who advocate the Sabbath as the correct day of worship to God claim that the Ten Commandments are everlasting and that they were binding before Moses received them at Sinai. Nehemiah, however, contradicts that very idea when he said, "

> You came down on mount Sinai, and spoke with them from Heaven, and gave them right judgments and true laws, good statutes and commandments. You made known to them your holy Sabbath, and commanded them commandments, statutes, and laws, by the hand of Moses Your servant." (Neh 9:13–14)

Moses also confirms that the Ten Commandments were given at Sinai when he said, "The Lord our God made a covenant with us in Horeb. The Lord made not this covenant with our fathers; but with us, even us, who are all of us here alive this day" (Deut 5:2–3). Moses follows this proclamation by immediately repeating the Ten Commandments as embodying the covenant that was made with them and not their fathers before them. The reason for giving the Sabbath is stated in Exodus 31:12–14. It was given as a sign to Israel between the nation and God. It was not a sign for the generations before Sinai, nor for the time after the inauguration of the new covenant by the blood of

Jesus. Take careful note of these New Testament passages:

> For he is our peace, he, making us both one, and he has broken down the middle wall of partition between us, having abolished in his flesh the enmity (the Law of commandments contained in ordinances) so that in himself he might make the two into one new man, making peace between them. (Eph 2:14–15)

> Blotting out the handwriting of ordinances that was against us, which was contrary to us, and has taken it out of the way, nailing it to the cross. Having stripped rulers and authorities, he made a show of them publicly, triumphing over them in it. Therefore let no one judge you in food or in drink, or in respect of a feast, or of the new moon, or of the sabbaths. For these are a shadow of things to come, but the body is of Christ. (Col 2:14–17)

> But now he has obtained a more excellent ministry, by so much he is also the mediator of a better covenant, which was built upon better promises. For if that first covenant had been without fault, then no place would have been sought for the second. For finding fault with them, he said to them, 'Behold, days are coming, says the Lord, and I will make an end on the house of Israel and on the house of

> Judah; a new covenant shall be, not according to the covenant that I made with their fathers in the day I took hold of their hand to lead them out of the land of Egypt.' In that he says, a new covenant, he has made the first one old. Now that which decays and becomes old is ready to vanish away. (Heb 8:6–13)

There is no truth more plainly taught in the Scriptures than the fact that the Sinai Law was insufficient and that it was replaced by a new and better law—the Law of Christ; a new and better covenant (Heb 8:6; 12:24).

Application

Under the new covenant, which is for Jews and Gentiles, we have new rules and practices. The Law of Moses was for the nation of the Jews only. Under the new covenant, we follow the rules and practices that were given for the new Israel—the church that was bought with the blood of Christ. The early church was worshipping the Lord on the first day of the week, not the seventh (Sabbath). The church broke bread (the Lord's supper) on the "first day of the week" (Acts 20:7). The Corinthian church was coming together on the "first day of the week" for something special; therefore, they were to give on the first day of the week (1 Cor 16:2). John refers to the special day as the "Lord's day" (Rev 1:10). We have three references from the New

Testament that the Christian's day of worship was the first day of the week or "the Lord's Day" as it was called by inspired men.

We follow the early church's example and worship on the day of the week when our Lord was raised, not the day that God set as a sign to the ancient nation of Israel. The first day of the week is the day God confirmed as our day of worship when he brought forth his Son from the sealed tomb as our risen Savior, Priest, and King. The church was established on the first day of the week in accordance to Leviticus 23:15–16:

> And you shall count to you from the next day after the sabbath, from the day that you brought the sheaf of the wave offering; seven sabbaths shall be complete. To the next day after the seventh sabbath you shall number fifty days. And you shall offer a new food offering to Jehovah.

The fiftieth day (Pentecost) was the first day of the week. The most important events in the New Testament were connected to the first day of the week.

Discussion

1. Why was the Sabbath sacred to the Jews?
2. Why is the Sabbath not a sacred day to New Testament Christians?

3. Why is the first day of the week the special day of remembrance and worship for Christians?
4. Is Sunday to be treated with the Sabbath restrictions and regulations?

8. HONORING PARENTS
PHILIP GOAD

Ephesians 6:1–3

One Main Thing

Imagine how much stronger our families, the church, and even our culture could be today if the fifth commandment were better embraced and followed!

Introduction

Many would agree that the erosion of God's structure for the family is a huge factor in God's not being respected and in so many of the challenges our society faces today. Well over a century ago, Alexander McLaren stated the following as he wrote about the fifth commandment: "No more serious damage can be inflicted on society or on individuals than the weakening of the honour paid to fathers and mothers."[1]

Scripture reveals the importance of this commandment, and it still needs our attention today.

Going Deeper

Exodus 20:12 states, "Honor your father and your mother, that your days may be prolonged in the land which the Lord your God gives you." As the fifth word or commandment, this instruction seems to serve as a transition. The first four commandments concern man's responsibilities to God, and the last five deal with man's responsibilities to fellow man. Scholars have debated whether the fifth commandment belongs with the first four or with the last five. The case can be made that honor for parents has more to do with honoring God than it does with honoring fellow man.

Consider the responsibilities that God has delegated to parents. Obviously, the care and protection of children are paramount. It's worth noting that humans take much longer to become self-supporting than other species. Perhaps one of the reasons is that there is so much that a child needs to learn from his/her parents. God's plan is that parents teach their children about life and, more importantly, about God. By way of parents, children begin to learn about right and wrong in what they hear and see. The inspired words found in Deuteronomy 6 are familiar. After reminding God's people to love the Lord "with all your heart and with all your soul and with all your mind" (v. 5), Moses then emphasizes that all of these commands must be taught diligently to children (vv. 6–9). Because of all that parents do to begin connecting children to God, showing honor for parents helps children better understand the need to honor God.

The word translated "honor" in both Exodus 20 and Deuteronomy 5 "derives from a root word meaning 'weighty' (in terms of impressiveness or importance) and is often used to refer to the glory of God."[2] On the other hand, Leviticus 19:3 admonishes, "Every one of you shall reverence his mother and his father," using a different word (translated here "reverence"), that sometimes describes literal fear (Gen 19:3) and at other times indicates a healthy fear of, or respect for, God (Exod 1:17). There can be no doubt that God intended for children to hold parents in high regard. There was even the promise of prolonged days as a people when this command was followed (Exod 20:12; Deut 5:16).

What else does Scripture teach us about the fifth commandment?

God placed great importance on this commandment. The stubborn and rebellious child who refused to honor his/her parents was an "evil" that needed to be removed (Deut 21:18–21). Striking or cursing one's father or mother were also dishonorable acts punishable by death (Exod 21:15, 17). And, while the severe consequences for violating the command don't appear in the New Testament, the instruction to be obedient and show honor certainly do (Eph 6:1–3).

Children seemingly don't outgrow the need to observe this command. Deuteronomy 21:20 refers to the disobedient child as being a "glutton and a drunkard." It seems that the child must be at least close to adulthood to be described this way. The same idea is present in Exodus 21 related to the child who would strike or curse his/her parents. Proverbs 23:22 states, "… and do not despise your mother when she is old." The word "despise" carries with it the idea of disrespect—the opposite of showing honor. Again, if momma is now old, the child is likely an adult.

Following parental teaching typically leads to a better life. While showing honor for parents includes more than just obedience to them, Solomon included some important teaching about the value of obedience in Proverbs 6:20–23. As he writes about obedience and continually leaning in to what parents have taught, he states that parental teaching will provide guidance, protection, and a constant reminder about how to do life. In verse 23, he refers to the reproofs of parental discipline as being "the way of life." Later in Proverbs, Solomon would state that every child's goal should be for his/her parents to rejoice and be glad when they think about the child they have raised (23:24–25).

Honor for parents may include providing for them monetarily. In the first part of Matthew 15, Jesus is exposing the false teaching of the Pharisees and scribes. In doing so, he uses the fifth commandment as a teaching example. These corrupt Jewish leaders were

Honoring Parents

permitting the person who didn't want to help his parents financially to state that the money that would have been used for that purpose had been given to God (v. 5). Jesus told them they had, "invalidated the word of God for the sake of your tradition" (v. 6). It's hardly surprising that in the very next verse, Jesus refers to these Jewish leaders as hypocrites. Later, during his lowest personal moment, while hanging on the cross, Jesus remembers to make sure that his mother, Mary, would be taken care of. After his statements to his mother and to John, the Bible states that John took her into his home from that day forward (John 19:26–27).

Application

So how can we better follow this commandment as we do life in the twenty-first century? This question becomes especially important when so many today are faced with family situations that differ from God's blueprint for the home. Many homes today are broken in some way. Some Christians have found a relationship with Jesus despite having not been raised by Christian parents. Some Christians have parents whose lives don't seem worthy of honor. Some adult children carry the burden of previous dishonor that has scarred the relationship with parents.

No matter the circumstance, it seems that the appropriate response must be to determine to live biblically and to only attempt to control the things that one can control. As we do, we can take heart in remembering that many of the families we read about in Scripture were dysfunctional in some way. Following are some suggestions:

- I can determine to do everything within my power to produce a family environment that is consistent with God's plan. Yes, my family may already be scarred or broken, but as a parent, I can determine that my children will see me honoring God. How will they see this? They will see this when I make my best effort to live obediently in all aspects of my life. They will experience this when I teach them to honor God with their lives as well (Eph 6:1–4). By determining to live obediently, I position myself as the kind of parent that my children should find easy to honor.
- I can choose to show honor to my parents, no matter what my age or stage of life. Even if my parents are living or have lived in a way that seemingly doesn't honor God, I can honor them as a function of showing honor for God. As I seek to live obediently, it is also important for my children to see me showing honor to my parents. Children learn by example. And remember this: no matter how strained a current relationship

Honoring Parents

may be with my parents, I should still want to see them eventually come to salvation. While there is life, there remains the hope of successful evangelism. Finally, even if my parents have passed, I can still choose to honor them by making decisions that show honor to God.

Conclusion

Without question, the fifth commandment still needs the attention of every God-seeking person today. Through embracing God's instruction to show honor for parents, homes can be strengthened, life here can be better, and more people can end up in heaven.

Discussion

1. How is showing honor for parents also a way of showing honor for God?
2. What are some of the main causes for children choosing to not show honor for parents in our world today? What can be done to change it?
3. Is a broken home a reasonable excuse for ignoring the fifth commandment? Why or why not?
4. Does it seem that some parents today are

counting on the church to teach the children things that should be taught at home?
5. What is the role of the church in producing spiritually healthy families?

Endnotes

1. Alexander Maclaren, *Genesis to Numbers* (17 vols.; Expositions of Holy Scripture; 1904-1910; repr., Grand Rapids: Baker, 1982), 1:111.

2. John J. Parsons, "Aseret Hadiberot – The Fifth Commandment," n.p. [undated]. Online:

http://www.hebrew4christians.com/Scripture/Torah/Ten_Cmds/Fifth_Cmd/fifth_cmd.html.

9. AGAINST MURDER
BRAD MCKINNON

MATTHEW 5:21–24

One Main Thing

The baseline for how we are to treat each other is found in the ancient admonition, "You Shall Not Murder."

Introduction

There are many examples of ancient law codes that prohibited murder. Early Mesopotamian civilizations, such as Sumer, Babylon, and Assyria all had them. For instance, the Sumerian Code of Ur-Nammu (ca. 2100 BC) includes a rather straightforward injunction against murder and the subsequent punishment: "If a man commits a murder, that man must be killed."[1] Developing out of a similar cultural context, it shouldn't surprise us that ancient Israel emphasized the protection of human life as well.

Going Deeper

The Sixth Commandment in Translation

The traditional rendering, "Thou shalt not kill," has been replaced in most modern translations with something like, "You shall not murder" (Exod 20:13; NRSV). Legally, the term *murder* has a very specific connotation—the unlawful and usually intentional taking of a human life. There are other terms (i.e. manslaughter) that indicate unlawful killing that is unintentional or without premeditation. So, the initial question for the student of Scripture is whether or not the Hebrew word (*ratsah*) allows for the narrowing of the prohibition so that it would not include killing that may be intentional, but legal, such as capital punishment, killing in combat, etc.

A quick perusal of other passages where the term *ratsah* appears indicates the term can include a meaning broader than "murder." While in Exodus, the term occurs only in 20:13, it turns up quite often elsewhere in the Pentateuch, almost exclusively in relation to the establishment of cities of refuge. In Numbers 35:11 for instance, to justify the need for such cities, the term describes one who kills "in error" or unintentionally.

However, when it comes to the notion of killing as

punishment for a crime or in an act of war, another term (*muth*) is typically used to indicate putting someone to death (Num 35:12; Deut 20:5). So, while the term *ratsah* cannot be so rigidly translated to rule out all unintentional killing, the language within the Pentateuch itself indicates that the use of the English term "murder" instead of "kill" seems justified.

The Sixth Commandment in Context

A simple way of organizing the Ten Commandments or Ten Words is to think about them both vertically and horizontally in terms of our responsibilities toward God (vertical) and our responsibilities toward people (horizontal). Our duty toward God comes first —"You shall have no other gods before me," etc. Our obligations toward people then radiate from this acknowledgment of God.[2] These expectations begin naturally with our earliest interpersonal connections —namely the relationship we have with our parents— "Honor your father and your mother." However, as we grow up, we gradually begin interacting with people beyond the safe space (hopefully) of life with Mom and Dad.

Once we begin relating to people outside the primal familial relationship, the baseline ethic is "You shall not murder." And this makes sense within the broader context of the Five Books of Moses. After all, the archetypical murder in the biblical text happens in a relationship just outside the parental one (Gen 4:1–16).

The Sixth Commandment in the Sermon on the Mount

In Matthew's Gospel, Jesus often seems to be depicted as more or less a new Moses. Soon after his birth, for instance, Jesus is hidden from an evil ruler (King Herod) who seeks to kill him, just like Moses was protected from pharaoh. In the process, the king orders male children to be killed. Also, Jesus travels to and from Egypt, and he spends forty days and forty nights in the wilderness, like Moses wandered in the Sinai Peninsula for forty years. So, it shouldn't surprise us that when Jesus begins his public ministry, his opening words in Matt 5:1–12 sound a lot like a new Ten Commandments.

After the Beatitudes, Jesus focuses attention on the Torah, noting that expert interpretations of the commandments, many handed down for generations, were incomplete. Jesus agreed murder was prohibited by the Law, and one who violated the injunction was "liable to judgment" (Matt 5:21). However, there were deeper processes at work. Jesus sought to get to the heart of the matter—to determine why killing often takes place in the first place.

According to the Federal Bureau of Investigation, the majority of people murdered in the United States are killed by people known to them.[3] Jesus underscores just those kinds of scenarios, because those are the sorts of situations that we have the opportunity to rectify simply by the way we think, feel, and act. For instance, Jesus speaks of not being angry with your brother or sister. Just like the murderer was liable to judgment, so too was the one so consumed by his or her anger that it could lead to violence. Now, it's important to understand that Jesus isn't condemning all anger. Jesus often got quite angry, especially in response to injustice committed against others (Matt 21:12–13). However, he didn't lash out in anger in response to personal slights and insults (Matt 5:39). Recognizing both types of anger, the Apostle Paul encouraged the Ephesians, "Be angry but do not sin; do not let the sun go down on your anger" (Eph 4:26).

Jesus also warns against insulting a brother or sister. Often the kind of anger that leads to violence includes dehumanizing your rivals. Words like "fool," "idiot," and much worse have a tendency to do this. And, finally, in a context of judicial proceedings, he recommends coming to terms quickly with any adversaries one may have. Here, Jesus recognizes the importance of peaceful resolutions of personal disputes.

Application

You can tell by even a quick glance at the Ten Commandments that some are stated positively ("You shall ...) and some are stated negatively ("You shall not ..."). A helpful exercise is to take the "negative" commandments and to restate them positively.[4] This is what Martin Luther attempted to do in his *Small Catechism* (1529). Regarding this commandment, Luther observes that "You are not to kill" means: "We are to fear and love God, so that we neither endanger nor harm the lives of our neighbors, but instead help and support them in all of life's needs."[5]

A few things from Luther's analysis stand out. First, he connects the relationships we have with other people to our relationship with God, thus integrating the horizontal with the vertical (or the extraordinary with the ordinary). It's our respect and love for God as a transcendent being that drives our ordinary relationships. Heavenly things cannot be detached from earthly things. Second, Luther describes the relationships we have with others in terms of a relationship between neighbors. This brings to mind Jesus's admonition embedded in the Parable of the Good Samaritan. In the story, the priest and the Levite did no actual harm to the wounded man; it was the robbers that left him "half dead" (Luke 10:30). But, the designation *neighbor* was reserved for the Samaritan—the one who did active good. Thus, Luther argues that we should not only avoid doing physical harm to others, but we should actively ease others' material needs.

Conclusion

I would imagine that very few of us would ever be tempted to actually take another's life—much less carry it out. However, the admonition, "You shall not murder," is more complex than that. Avoiding murder is simply the baseline of the ethical demands God places on us—not the ceiling. Our lives must be characterized by active good in the lives of others. Am I helping provide food, clothing, and shelter to those in need? Am I promoting an atmosphere of forgiveness, justice, and peace in my community and the world? Or am I satisfied with just being able to say that I did no harm? Regarding mercy, Jesus charged, "Go and do likewise" (Luke 10:37).

Discussion

1. Explain the significance of the updated translation: "You shall not murder" (Exod 20:13).
2. How do you think your relationship with God can be affected by your relationships with others?
3. Why do you think Jesus links murder with anger, insults, and personal disputes?
4. How would you restate the sixth commandment positively?
5. List some ways you can actively demonstrate how much you value human life.

Endnotes

1. Code of Ur-Nammu.

   http://www.polk.k12.ga.us/userfiles/644/Classes/177912/Code%20of%20Ur-Nammu.pdf.

2. For more on this idea, see the first lesson in this book.

3. U.S. Federal Bureau of Investigation. 2011. *Crime in the United States.*

   https://ucr.fbi.gov/crime-in-the-u.s/2011/crime-in-the-u.s.-2011/offenses-known-to-law-enforcement/expanded/expanded-homicide-data.

4. Keith Stanglin, "No Other Gods," Christian Studies (blog), Austin Graduate School of Theology, February 10, 2018.

   http://info.austingrad.edu/christianstudies/chronicler-as-writer-0.

5. Robert Kolb and Timothy J. Wengert, eds., *The Book of Concord: The Confessions of the Evangelical Lutheran Church* (Minneapolis: Fortress Press, 2000), 352.

10. AGAINST ADULTERY
MICHAEL JACKSON

Exodus 20:14

One Main Thing

God's seventh commandment that we should not commit adultery is rooted in the nature of God himself and has sobering implications for the way Christians honor their marriage vows.

Introduction

Adultery is mentioned more than 40 times in more than 35 verses of most modern English translations of the Bible. But what exactly is adultery? Adultery is voluntary sexual intercourse by someone in a married relationship with someone else who is not his or her marriage partner, which is regarded as a violation of the marriage vows.[1] The biblical record reveals further descriptions of this definition.

In the Old Testament, we find that adultery is not only limited to a sexual relationship after marriage, but also includes someone who is betrothed (engaged in a contract of marriage; Deut 22:23–24). The penalty for adultery according to the Torah is death (Lev 20:10; cf. John 8:1–11), indicating the seriousness with which the sin was taken. The evidence is mixed on how consistently this punishment was carried out in Israel. The seriousness of the sin of adultery may also explain the grouping of this commandment with murder and stealing in the order of the Ten Commandments and elsewhere in Scripture (Jer 7:9; Hos 4:2).

In the New Testament, Jesus reveals his divine understanding of the commandment:

> You have heard that it was said, "You shall not commit adultery"; but I say to you that everyone who looks at a woman with lust for her has already committed adultery with her in his heart. If your right eye makes you stumble, tear it out and throw it from you; for it is better for you to lose one of the parts of your body, than for your whole body to be thrown into hell. If your right hand makes you stumble, cut it off and throw it from you; for it is better for you to lose one of the parts of your body, than for your whole body to go into hell. (Matt 5:27–30)

Jesus's insight into adultery broadens our understanding of where adultery begins (in the heart) and deepens our appreciation for just how seriously we should take the biblical instruction against it (hell is not worth whatever gratification adultery may bring).

Going Deeper

Why does God so expressly forbid violation of the marriage vows with such serious consequences? This has been a question of interest to scholars and Christians. Understanding why God commands what he commands leads us on an important journey in equipping ourselves to live the way he desires for us to live. Here are some explanations that have been put forward:

Mistaken paternity.[2] It is suggested that Israelite society strongly depended upon the knowledge of who a child's father was. Without a paternal guarantee, an illegitimate heir could be given the family inheritance and be expected to carry on the family name. Even though the father might not know of this infidelity, his family name could become extinct. Leviticus 20:20–21 demonstrates the social importance of the concept of family extinction in Israel by stating that childlessness will follow those men that commit adultery with their close relatives. In addition, children of illicit unions were not allowed into the worship assembly (Deut 23:2).

Economic violation. It has also been suggested that in a patriarchy like Israel, women and children were under the responsibility of fathers/husbands, and thus a property violation occurs in the transaction of adultery. While there is no doubt that Israel was a patriarchal society, this view receives less attention in the biblical texts on adultery (but see Exod 22:16–17).

Violation of exclusive sexual rights.[3] Husbands in Israel were considered to be the guardians of their wives' sexuality, and therefore exclusively entitled to it. This is why, when adultery is condemned in certain parts of the Torah, it is expressly stated as a transgression against the husband of the woman caught in adultery (Deut 22:24).

Violation of creation. The Bible portrays the union of man and woman into one flesh as divinely ordered for the benefit of both parties (Gen 2:18, 23–24). It is clearly indicated in those passages that there is an intimacy in the union of man and woman to one another, addressing loneliness, meeting needs, and ushering in a transition from childhood to adulthood. In this design, man is fruitful and multiplies (Gen 1:28). Perhaps more importantly, the image of God is reproduced in the world when his purposes for man and woman are followed (Gen 1:27).

While we certainly recognize the importance of the social consequences of illegitimate heirs in a patrilineal (property and title are inherited by the male lineage) society, the true key to understanding God's heart in the commandment to abstain from adultery is found through an understanding of points 3 and 4, especially when these are seen as flowing from the very nature of God himself.

God Desires Our Exclusive Allegiance. As you have already learned in this study, the Ten Commandments begin with a reminder of our responsibility to be faithful exclusively to God. It makes sense, then, that God desires for us to honor our vows of faithfulness in the covenant of marriage. This connection does not only make sense logically, it is metaphorically referenced in passages in Scripture where adultery is used as imagery for spiritual unfaithfulness.

> Why should I pardon you? Your sons have forsaken Me and sworn by those who are not gods. When I had fed them to the full, they committed adultery and trooped to the harlot's house. (Jer 5:7)

> Harlotry, wine and new wine take away the understanding. My people consult their wooden idol, and their diviner's wand informs them; For a spirit of harlotry has led them astray, and they have played the harlot, departing from their God. They offer sacrifices on the tops of the mountains and burn incense on the hills, under oak, poplar and terebinth, because their shade is pleasant. Therefore, your daughters play the harlot and your brides commit adultery. I will not punish your

> daughters when they play the harlot or your brides when they commit adultery, for the men themselves go apart with harlots and offer sacrifices with temple prostitutes; so the people without understanding are ruined. (Hos 4:11–14)

The nature and character of God requires allegiance to our covenants and vows to him as well as to our fellow man and—in the case of adultery specifically—our spouse.

God's Created Order Is Purposeful in Its Design. Jesus appealed to the created order as proof of God's intention for how man and woman were to dwell in the union of marriage together (Matt 19:4–6). Paul extends this order to our understanding of Christ himself and his relationship to the Church (Eph 5:22–33).

If we wish to understand why God so expressly forbids the violation of marriage vows, and why the punishments for those violations are grave and severe, then we must first endeavor to understand how important it is to God that we pledge total allegiance and fidelity to the covenants we make. And, we must understand that marriage itself is based in the nature and character of God's created order, which provides us a better way of understanding Christ himself and his relationship to the church.

Application

I'm reminded of a news story I recently saw about a politician who had just been sworn into office. The headline read, "Jordan Intends to Keep His Vows." The headline engenders sober reflection, even though it is intended to be positive. Is it news in today's world to keep the promises we've made? It is a struggle that we all face.

Jesus knew this. He teaches us over and over that we should honor our word and commitments (Matt 5:33–37; 7:21–23; 12:36–37). Why is this so important? Because God himself is faithful. He expects our lives to be lived in light of that truth.

And yet life brings challenges that strike at the very core of our identity, testing our commitments and our intentions: the death of a loved one, the loss of a job, the joys and struggles of children and parenthood, and/or health problems, etc. Those who are married often find themselves reconsidering their marriage vows, though they may have made those vows sincerely at the time. God desires that during those times of reevaluation, we reaffirm our vows.

> Marriage is to be held in honor among all, and the marriage bed is to be undefiled; for fornicators and adulterers God will judge. (Heb 13:4)

Conclusion

Faithfulness to God is shown in our faithfulness to one another. This is nowhere more important or evident than in the way we honor the commitment of marriage. Adultery is expressly forbidden by the seventh commandment and shown throughout Scripture to be in violation of God's image for his children. We as God's children must endeavor to be faithful in all things with him as our help and guide.

Discussion

1. What do the passages referenced from the Old Testament teach us about God's views on adultery and transgressing the seventh commandment?
2. What insights do Jesus's words in the Sermon on the Mount give us to help us understand how adultery
3. Why do you believe that God so expressly forbids violation of the marriage vows and invokes such serious consequences?
4. How does an understanding of God's creation and the relationship of Christ to the church help us to understand our marriage vows and their significance?
5. What strategies might we use to help us

hold to our commitments in those times
when life stretches them to their limits?

Endnotes

1. *Oxford English Dictionary* (http://www.oed.com/), entry "Adultery," definition 1a.

2. *Anchor Bible Dictionary,* ed. D. N. Freedman (New York: Doubleday, 1992), entry "Adultery," section A.

3. *Dictionary of Scripture and Ethics*, ed. J. B. Green (Grand Rapids: Baker, 2011), entry "Adultery."

11. AGAINST STEALING
MATT HEUPEL

Ephesians 4:28

One Main Thing

Respecting the property of others is one of the fundamental principles of law and government. Within the eighth commandment, God has provided for us a provision of enforcing that principle.

Introduction

Becoming the heirs of the Promise of Abraham must have certainly been an honor, as well as a blessing, for the nation of Israel. However, that did not exempt God's people from sin and temptation. The people were still a people who had shortcomings and faults; therefore, God had to institute some aspect of Law to keep them accountable to Him. These laws were a way

Against Stealing

that God could protect the sanctity of their relationship with Him, as well as promote a healthy relationship between each other. The commandment, under consideration for this chapter, is "Thou shalt not steal." I am sure that when those words were repeated by Moses on the mountain, the Israelites were not surprised by this eighth commandment. The theft of property, as a crime, has probably been a part of every form of law and government that has ever existed. It has, it is, and it will always continue to be a problem for any group of individuals that are living in some type of community this side of Heaven.

According to a 2016 study conducted by the Federal Bureau of Investigation on Crime in the United States, it was reported that the value of items reported stolen was estimated at $13,667,503,625. These reported thefts represent a wide spectrum of items, from stolen cars to stolen corn. If you have ever had something stolen from you, you understand that the amount of loss financially is important, but isn't usually that significant. No matter what the value of the loss, you feel somewhat disrespected and, in a strange way, even violated.

Going Deeper

Although the command from God seems to be clear, we have found a way to cloud that clarity through rationalization. Let me explain. If one were to shoplift from a department store, that action is clearly a violation of the command. However, one may use a questionable deduction on a tax form to get a better refund by rationalizing that the IRS gets enough from us as it is. Both instances are a violation of the commandment. To steal means to thieve, to deceive, to secretly obtain or to get by stealthily." Jeremiah 17:9 tells us "The heart is deceitful above all things, and desperately sick; who can understand it?" Our heart sometimes can cloud and deceive our understanding based on the circumstances. Again, it isn't the amount that was taken that makes this a violation, but the fact that something was taken through deceitful means.

It is also important to understand that theft is not just about money. Under the Law, stealing involves the moving of property boundaries (Deut 19:14), the inaccuracy of measuring weights and balances (Lev 19:35–36), dealing falsely with one another (Lev 19:11), kidnapping (Exod 21:16), and not returning something found that is not yours (Exod 23:4). We must understand that anything taken by means of deceiving others classifies as stealing.

Stealing isn't something only committed against your fellow man. It is also possible to steal from God. The Bible tells us that God has created all things and that all things are his. As the pinnacle of his creation, he has given us the responsibility of being stewards of this creation. Part of that responsibility of stewardship is the giving back of our first fruits to God. It is God's way of reminding us that all things are his and without him we would have nothing. By withholding that portion that God has asked for, we are keeping something that belongs to him, robbing from God. Malachi illustrated this concept (Mal 3:8–9). The same is also true of our talents and abilities with which God has blessed us. By not using them in his service, we are withholding something that rightfully belongs to him. For example, perhaps my neighbor lends me his rake to dispose of my leaves. Instead of returning the rake when finished, I might keep it in my garage. When I see my neighbor the next week outside attempting to dispose of his leaves without a rake, if I refuse to return his rake to him, am I not in the wrong? I am withholding something that is rightfully his—stealing from my neighbor. Is it not therefore the same thing for me to use my talents for personal gain, yet when given the opportunity to use it for God, refuse? In doing so I am withholding something that God gave me and not giving back to him when he requires it, thus stealing from God.

Application

The prohibition of stealing wasn't just a law for the nation of Israel. The same command is reiterated in the New Testament. Paul places it in the same category as idolatry and adultery in his letter to the Corinthians.

> Do not be deceived: neither the sexually immoral, nor idolaters, nor adulterers, nor men who practice homosexuality, nor thieves, nor the greedy, nor drunkards, nor revilers, nor swindlers will inherit the kingdom of God. (1 Cor 6:9–10)

Paul also condemns withholding of things owed, in his letter to the Romans "Pay to all what is owed to them: taxes to whom taxes are owed, revenue to whom revenue is owed" (Rom 13:7). Finally, when Jesus summed up the whole Law in loving your neighbor as yourself, he included stealing in his conversation with the Rich Young Ruler (Matt 19:16–19). These accounts help us to understand that stealing was considered a sin in the Old Testament as well as in the New Testament.

But what does the prohibition against stealing have to do with us in the twenty-first century? Not only does the commandment affect us in the sense that we should not commit the act of thievery, but it also helps do a few other things.

In our obedience to the command of not stealing, we are condemning selfishness. Selfishness is one of the greatest factors of the sin of stealing. A person sees something he wants, he takes it. There is no concern for the loss of the person from which the thing was taken, only a short-term sense of gratification due to acquiring something for free. That is the very definition of selfishness: caring only for oneself, one's own interests or welfare regardless of others. Paul reminds the church at Philippi that when we are only concerned about ourselves, we are not imitating Christ (Phil 2:3–11). In our efforts not to steal, we are taking those thoughts of greed, desire, and selfishness captive to obey Christ (2 Cor 10:5).

In our efforts of condemning selfishness, we establish a foundation to promote unity. If James is correct in saying that jealousy and selfishness bring "disorder and every vile practice" (Jas 3:16), then the omission of such things should foster unity and generosity. Paul urged those from the church of Ephesus, who had been guilty of stealing, to stop and use their talents to help others. "Let the thief no longer steal, but rather let him labor, doing honest work with his own hands, so that he may have something to share with anyone in need" (Eph 4:28). God wants to turn thieves into productive members of society by helping those who might be tempted to steal. When we respect the property of others and focus our efforts in honest work, society profits and becomes more unified. If we simply followed the Golden Rule (Matt 7:12), the number of burglaries would go down and the amount of generosity shown to others would go up.

Our obedience to the eighth commandment also helps us maintain a proper perspective on the ownership of things. Moses once said, "Behold, to the LORD your God belong heaven and the heaven of heavens, the earth with all that is in it" (Deut 10:14). The New

Testament echoes the same sentiment: "the earth is the Lord's, and the fullness thereof" (1 Cor 10:26). Everything in this world belongs to God and we encourage recognition of this fact when we refuse to violate the eighth commandment. We do not want to find ourselves robbing God (Mal 3:8–9).

Conclusion

Let's encourage one another to refrain from stealing by reflecting on these two verses.

> Seek ye first the kingdom of God and His righteousness, and all these things will be given unto you. (Matt 6:33)

> Keep your life free from love of money, and be content with what you have, for he has said, "I will never leave you nor forsake you" (Heb 13:5).

Discussion

1. What are some ways people violate the eighth commandment?
2. How is it possible to "rob God"?
3. What must we do to prevent ourselves and others from violating the eighth commandment?

12. AGAINST LYING
TRAVIS HARMON

Matthew 5:37

One Main Thing

We have to learn how to be honest. By nature, we tend to default to dishonesty when under pressure or when we want a pleasure we cannot otherwise have.

Introduction

The ninth commandment is a prohibition against dishonesty: "You shall not bear false witness against your neighbor" (Exod 20:16). Under the Mosaic Law, the court system was based on testimony of witnesses. The integrity of the system was only as sure as the integrity of the participants. It was an absolute necessity that those involved be honest. Of course, the command is more far-reaching than just official court function. In general, those who fear God should not make false statements. God wants for us to be people of the highest moral integrity. To do that, we have to work at it. We have to learn to trust God and obey his commands even when we think we see a shortcut to getting what we want. God says that honesty is not the best policy; it is the only policy.

Going Deeper

Psalm 51 is one of the most beautiful passages in all of Scripture. David, after his sin, cries out to God and asks for forgiveness. The emotions are raw and powerful, and the imagery is magical and poetic. Seeing this glimpse into David's heart is amazing and beautiful. However, Psalm 51:5 is also one of the most hotly debated passages in all of Scripture. Some people have said that this verse—"Behold, I was brought forth in iniquity; and in sin did my mother conceive me"—teaches that we are sinful from birth. David is not saying that we are born into sin. David is saying that he was born a sinner. This has nothing to do with inherited sin. This is an example of hyperbole. Hyperbole is a rhetorical device in which a person makes an exaggerated claim to make a point.

David is saying that he is a horrible person, and he is attempting to communicate that concept poetically by exaggerating. David is just saying that he feels like he is bad, very bad. He is not teaching that babies are born sinful. He is not teaching a doctrine. He is simply making a point about the amount of guilt he feels.

The same thing happens in Psalm 58:3, "The wicked are estranged from the womb; They go astray as soon as they are born, speaking lies." Obviously, babies do not come out of the womb with the ability to spread lies. Babies can't talk. We understand that the verse is not literal. Babies have to learn to talk, and they have to learn to lie before they can spread lies. The verse communicates how wicked some people can be by presenting this odd image of a little baby fresh from the womb telling lies. It is hard to be sure if the imagery is supposed to be more comical or horrifying, but it is certainly provocative and memorable.

A funny thing happens to parents. At some point, they realize that their child has learned to lie. Every parent has that story that they can tell about when they caught their sweet, innocent toddler in a bold-faced lie. This occurs shockingly earlier than you would think. Parents will tell you how they can ask their not-yet-verbal toddler a question and the toddler can knowingly lie by shaking his/her head.

There have been numerous studies that attempt to identify just when a child learns the art of deception. It is really a self-taught skill, even if the behavior has not been modeled for us. A child knows he is not supposed to be in the cookie jar but does it anyway. Maybe he leaves the lid off the jar and a chair pushed up to the counter. Mom asks the child if he got in the cookie jar.

Knowing that if he answers affirmatively it will result in punishment, he says, "No." He gets away with it this time. Guess what he does next time? It does not take long before a child realizes he can lie and sometimes get away with it. Upon reflection, we may wonder just how much hyperbole David is using in Psalm 58. We are not born guilty, but we get there about as fast as we can.

Application

When you think about it, you really do not have to be taught to lie. You really do have to be taught not to lie. That is exactly what the ninth commandment does. God says, "Do not lie." Repeatedly. God tells us that we are not to deceive each other. We are to love truth, and we are to view lies as evil.

David is exaggerating about babies walking out of the womb lying, but we do learn to lie quickly and have to be told not to lie. Learning not to lie is much harder than learning to lie. Learning to lie is second nature to us. Learning not to lie is really difficult.

In Matthew 5:37, Jesus says, "But let your communication be, Yea, yea; Nay, nay: for whatsoever is more than these cometh of evil." What he wants is for us to just speak the truth and only the truth. In the context, he is talking about taking oaths. Why do people take oaths? Why do we have to "swear on the Bible" when we want people to know we are telling the truth?

Against Lying

Because we live in a society of liars, so we have to have some way to differentiate. The need to make oaths and promises proves that we lie.

In Colossians 3:8-10, the Bible says,

> But now ye also put off all these; anger, wrath, malice, blasphemy, filthy communication out of your mouth. Lie not one to another, seeing that ye have put off the old man with his deeds; and have put on the new man, which is renewed in knowledge after the image of him that created him.

We have to learn to be Christians. We have to learn to be Christ-like. So much of growing in Christ is learning to not do the thing that is most natural to us. For example, Jesus says that when someone insults us, we are not to strike back. That is a learned skill. We also have to learn not to lie. When we are in trouble, we may be able to get out of it by lying. It is hard to learn to take the lumps and tell the truth; that is not the natural reaction.

We have to learn that when the phone rings and someone else answers and says, "It's Bob," and we say, "Tell him I am not here," we have told a lie. We must learn that "little white lies" are still lies. We cannot do that.

We have to learn that when we say, "Yes. I will do that Monday," knowing that we will not do it on Monday, that is an empty promise. We have to learn that a promise that we do not intend to keep is a lie. We cannot do that.

We have to learn that when we tell our kids, "If you do that one more time, I am going to ground you!" that when they do that one more time, we have to ground them. We have to learn when we make empty threats, a threat we do not intend to keep, it is a lie. We cannot do that.

We have to learn that when we could just lie to our boss about something that will never be found out, that is lying. We have to learn that bending the truth is a lie. We cannot do that.

It is hard to learn not to lie, but we have to learn.

Conclusion

There is a kids' song that I hear people playfully singing sometimes. It is an attempt at humor by being really shocking. You may know it, too. It is sung to the tune of "Frère Jacques" ("Are You Sleeping?") and says:

> Revelation, Revelation
> Twenty-one eight. Twenty-one eight.
> If you lie you will fry.
> Burn, burn, burn. Burn, burn, burn.

Revelation 21:8 says,

Against Lying

> But the fearful, and unbelieving, and the abominable, and murderers, and whoremongers, and sorcerers, and idolaters, and all liars, shall have their part in the lake which burneth with fire and brimstone: which is the second death.

It is hard to not see exactly how God feels about liars after reading that verse. That is a heavy list of what we would call "big, black sins." That is a list of sins that many of us would never even be tempted by, but there is one among them that we all have to learn to avoid.

As parents, we eventually figure out that our child has learned to lie, and we have to spend a lifetime teaching them not to. That is what God does.

We have to be told not to lie, and we have to work hard to learn not to lie. We have been told, and we better work and learn. Psalm 58:3 is hyperbole, but Revelation 21:8 is not.

Discussion

1. When do you believe that we learn to lie? Can you think of a situation where a very small child lied?
2. What would happen if there was no prohibition against lying? What would the world be like if no one ever lied?

3. What are some specific ways we still need to learn not to lie? (omissions, half-truths, gossip, etc.)
4. In your words, what does Revelation 21:27 teach us about lies?
5. Was it wrong for David to exaggerate in the Psalms? Would it be wrong for someone to embellish on a resume? Is there a difference between these examples?

13. AGAINST COVETING
JUSTIN GUIN

Exodus 20:17, Deuteronomy 5:21

One Main Thing

Overcoming covetousness requires me to align my desires with the word of God.

Introduction

In Genesis 3, Satan, in the form of a serpent, appears in the biblical narrative. He is described as one who is "crafty," and his shrewdness is immediately on display. As he encounters Adam and Eve, he targets their human frailties in a couple of ways. First, he undermines the authoritative command of God. Notice Satan's question, "Did God actually say?" (v. 1) With God's command in question, he tempts them with something they desired namely to be like God. In Genesis 3:6 Eve saw the food was "good" and the "tree was desired to make one wise." Then, she and Adam take the fruit, eat it, and transgress God's command. Why? Their desire was not in line with the will of God. Instead, they were guided by the desires of the flesh and eyes, and the pride of life (1 John 2:16).

Desire is a neutral emotion. It can be either righteous or unrighteous, depending on whether it is aligned with God's direction. The tenth commandment deals with avoiding ungodly desires. The previous nine commandments address outward expressions of faithful obedience. The final command is distinct from the others as it concentrates on an internal struggle. Outward obedience alone was not sufficient. The heart of Israel must also conform to the moral principles of the Ten Commandments. In so doing, they would bring their desires in line with God's will.

Going Deeper

Most translations render Exodus 20:17 as, "You shall not covet." We associate covetousness with sinful behavior because of the instruction in the Bible for us to be on guard against it. However, coveting is not sinful. The Hebrew word *hamad* is accurately translated "to desire or delight in."[1] The ancient Greek translation (the Septuagint) uses *epithumeo* in Exodus

Against Coveting

20:17, which is most often rendered "to desire or long for something or someone."[2]

When does coveting become sinful? It becomes sinful when the object of our desire does not rightfully belong to us or is in direct violation of God's instruction. Thus, Moses qualifies the command: "You shall not covet your neighbor's house; you shall not covet your neighbor's wife, or his male servant, or his female servant, or his ox, or his donkey, or anything that is your neighbor's" (Exod 20:17). All of these are people and possessions, which belong to the household of another. They are in descending order of importance. Notice each particular in the Lord's command:

Neighbor's wife—she is given priority due to the sanctity of marriage and the danger of adultery.

Male and female servants—this desire is rooted in selfishness and materialism as more servants increased the estate of another person.

Livestock—among nomadic people, livestock demonstrated wealth. You must not increase your wealth by stealing or defrauding your neighbor.

Summary—anything that is your neighbor's possession is a "catch all" phrase to keep selfish desires in check.

To desire and to try to obtain the property of another is to be dissatisfied with what God has given, and thus to show lack of faith in his love.

A second focus in this command is the welfare of one's neighbor. Sinful desires violate the "second greatest command" to love your neighbor as yourself (Matt 22:39; cf. Lev 19:18). What people desire often determines what type society they will create. We should never desire to harm our neighbor by taking what is rightfully his. Loving your neighbor as yourself motivates you to contribute good to society, and acting on illicit desires undermines society's moral fiber. Unchecked desires leads to a violation of God's other commands in the Decalogue. Desiring another's possessions leads to stealing. Lusting after another man's wife could progress to adultery. Thus, the final command is of vital importance as each person much keep his/her desires within the parameters of the Law given by the Lord. Such would ensure both corporate and individual holiness.

Covetousness and the New Testament

In the New Testament, warnings against covetousness appear both in Jesus's teaching in the Gospels and in Paul's letters. These warnings remind us of the peril in valuing any earthly possession more than our relationship with God. In Matthew 6:24, Jesus states that a Christian cannot serve both God and material things. Paul twice describes covetousness as "idolatry" (Eph 5:5, Col 3:5).

The word "idolatry" is a compound word meaning one who worships an object as God. Only God is worthy of our reverence and devotion. Understanding the proper value of possessions is key to knowing the purpose of life. We are created to worship and serve God and not material, temporal things.

A parable that clearly makes this point is found in Luke 12:13–21. Jesus is approached by a man who wants the Lord to divide the man's inheritance with his brother. It appears the man feels defrauded by his brother. Jesus does not give the man a ruling. Instead, Jesus teaches him about the purpose of life and how this relates to possessions. Note Luke 12:15, "And he said to them, 'Take care, and be on your guard against all covetousness, for one's life does not consist in the abundance of his possessions.'" Following this, Jesus illustrates his point with a parable about a man who prepares for his future but not his death. God calls him a fool (v. 20) and those who follow his course of life will not be "rich toward God." In our materialistic culture, we must heed the words of Jesus and evaluate what we're making our first priority. Are we seeking to become more wealthy or more faithful as our chief pursuit?

Application

How do we apply the final of the ten commandments and its prohibition against covetousness? Our desires lead to choices, which characterize our lives. Thus, we must know how to combat this scheme of Satan. Note a few principles which might help us in our struggle with immoral desires.

First, we must remember the source and end result of unlawful desires. The final commandment is not a prohibition against coveting per se. It is prohibition against lust. Our adversary uses our passions to deceive us into taking the hook of sin (Jas 1:13–15). He "lures" and "entices" us by our desires (v. 13). When we act on them, it leads us down sin's path ending in death (vv. 14–15). As an example, consider Achan's folly in Joshua 7. In the previous chapter, Israel had conquered Jericho, and the Lord had commanded them to devote everything for destruction (6:16–17). In Joshua 7, Israel was defeated at Ai because someone in their camp took some of the devoted things. Joshua confronted Achan, and Achan responded, "when I saw among the spoil a beautiful cloak from Shinar, and 200 shekels of silver, and a bar of gold weighing 50 shekels, then I coveted them and took them. And see, they are hidden in the earth inside my tent, with the silver underneath" (Josh 7:21). Achan started with unlawful desire and ended in death.

Second, we must heed the New Testament's teaching on coveting as it relates to materialism. Our Western culture pressures us to acquire more possessions and wealth. A bigger house, a larger salary, and expensive vacations are the markers of success. Many people measure their self-worth by this fleeting standard.

Pursuing such things makes temporary possessions our idol (Eph 5:5, 3:5). The problem is not with things.

The issue is with us. Money and physical possessions are neutral, and we should use the things we have to glorify and serve the Lord (1 Tim 6:19–20).

The key to overcoming a covetous, materialistic heart is learning contentment. In Philippians, Paul gives three keys to contentment, which will help us with this struggle:

We must have the right purpose for our life (1:21). Paul states, "For me to live is Christ, and to die is gain." Our goal in life is not to attain possessions. Rather, it is to serve Christ with all our heart.

We must give our lives in ministry to others (2:3–4). Paul instructs us to put the interests of others before our own and to follow the example of Christ. Attending to this instruction helps curtail selfish desires, which might lead us down the path of covetousness.

We must have the right aspirations (3:3–8). Paul was an accomplished Jew with many accolades. He considered these things as "rubbish" in comparison to knowing Christ. There is nothing more valuable than our relationship with Christ. Such an attitude keeps our desires in line with God's will.

Conclusion

God has abundantly blessed each one of us, and we must be prayerful and thankful (Phil 4:6–7). It is not sinful to desire good things for your life. We must not, however, allow them to become our master. We must strive to keep our desires in line with God's instruction. This will enable us to glorify God and will keep us from suffering the consequences of other sinful pursuits.

Discussion

1. How does Exodus 20:17 help us apply the moral instructions found in the other nine commandments?
2. What are some biblical principles that will allow us to make sure we're aligning our desires with God's instruction?
3. How does covetousness often lead to other sinful behaviors?
4. How does covetousness (materialism) relate to idolatry?
5. How does contentment help us with this struggle?

Endnotes

1. R. Laird Harris, Gleason L. Archer Jr., and Bruce K. Waltke, eds., *Theological Wordbook of the Old Testament*, (Chicago: Moody Press, 1999), 294. In the Old Testament, *hamad* is used both positively—such as desiring

God's word (Ps 19:10)—and negatively (cf. Gen 3:6). The object desired determines whether the desire is sinful.

2. Johannes P. Louw and Eugene Albert Nida, *Greek-English Lexicon of the New Testament: Based on Semantic Domains* (New York: UBS, 1989), 1: 289.

BIBLIOGRAPHY

Babylonian Talmud. tractate Makkot, 23b–24a.

Braulik, Greg. "The Sequence of the Laws in Deuteronomy 12–26 and in the Decalogue." Pages 313–35 in *A Song of Power and the Power of Song: Essays on the Book of Deuteronomy*. ed. Duane L. Christensen. Winona Lake, IN: Eisenbrauns, 1993.

Catechism of the Catholic Church 2.3. available online:
http://www.vatican.va/archive/ENG0015/_INDEX.HTM

Code of Ur-Nammu.
http://www.polk.k12.ga.us/userfiles/644/Classes/177912/Code%20of%20Ur-Nammu.pdf.

Goodfriend, Elaine Adler. "Adultery." Pages 82–86 in vol. 1 of *The Anchor Bible Dictionary*. Edited by David Noel Freedman. 6 vols. New York: Doubleday, 1992.

Harris, R. Laird, Gleason L. Archer Jr., and Bruce K. Waltke, eds. *Theological Wordbook of the Old Testament.* Chicago: Moody Press, 1999.

Heffernan, Margaret. *Willful Blindness: Why We Ignore the Obvious at Our Peril.* New York: Bloomsbury USA, 2011.

Josephus. *Antiquities of the Jews* 3.90–92.

Kolb, Robert, and Timothy J. Wengert, eds., *The Book of Concord: The Confessions of the Evangelical Lutheran Church.* Minneapolis: Fortress Press, 2000.

Louw, Johannes P., and Eugene Albert Nida. *Greek-English Lexicon of the New Testament: Based on Semantic Domains.* New York: United Bible Society, 1989.

Luther, Martin. *Small Catechism.* available online: http://bookofconcord.org/smallcatechism.php#tencommandments.

Maclaren, Alexander. *Genesis to Numbers.* 17 vols.; Expositions of Holy Scripture; 1904-1910; repr., Grand Rapids: Baker, 1982.

Olson, Dennis T. "Adultery." Pages 43–44 in *Dictionary of Scripture and Ethics.* ed. Joel B. Green. Grand Rapids: Baker Academic, 2011.

Oxford English Dictionary (http://www.oed.com/), entry "Adultery," definition 1a.

Parsons, John J. "Aseret Hadiberot – The Fifth Commandment," n.p. [undated]. Online:
http://www.hebrew4christians.com/Scripture/Torah/Ten_Cmds/Fifth_Cmd/fifth_cmd.html.

Philo. *On the Decalogue.*

Stanglin, Keith. "No Other Gods," Christian Studies (blog), Austin Graduate School of Theology, February 10, 2018.
http://info.austingrad.edu/christianstudies/chronicler-as-writer-0

U.S. Federal Bureau of Investigation. 2011. *Crime in the United States.*
https://ucr.fbi.gov/crime-in-the-u.s/2011/crime-in-the-u.s.-2011/offenses-known-to-law-enforcement/expanded/expanded-homicide-data.

Zehavy, Tzvee, trans. *The Talmud of the Land of Israel: A Preliminary Translation and Explanation.* vol. 1: Berakhot. Chicago: University of Chicago Press, 1989.

Scripture Index

Old Testament
Genesis
1:1–11:26	23
1:26–27	56
1:27	84
1:28	84
2:3	59
2:18	84
2:23–24	84
3	105
3:1	105
3:6	106, 113
4:1–16	75
4:26	50
11:27–50:26	23
12:8	50
13:4	50
16:13	50
19:3	67
21:33	50

Exodus
1:1–18:27	23
1:17	67
2:23	23
3	35, 51
3:3–16	28
3:7–9	23
6:7	23
13	35
14:18	23
16–18	23
16:6	23
16:34	33
19–20	2, 32
19–34	33
19:1–Num 10:10	23
19:1–Num 36:13	23
19:3–6	12, 17–18
19:3–7	33
19:4–6	23, 34
19:5	38
19:5–6	23
19:6	34
19:8	35
19:8–15	34
19:16–19	35
19:20–25	34
20	2, 26, 28–29, 39, 52
20:1	3
20:1–2	25, 27
20:1–17	2–3
20:1–32:33	34
20:2	4, 23, 35

Scripture Index

20:3	4, 32, 36–37, 52	33:19	51
20:4	4	34	34
20:4–6	42	34:1	10
20:5	4, 38	34:4–7	23
20:6	4	34:14	38
20:7	4, 50–51, 54	34:28	3, 10, 27, 32
20:8	4, 59	40:33b–38	23
20:8–11	58	40:34–38	23
20:9	4, 59	**Leviticus**	
20:10	4	11:45	23
20:11	4–5, 59	19	7–8
20:12	5, 66–67	19:2	19, 23
20:13	5, 74, 79	19:3	23, 67
20:14	5, 81	19:3–37	19
20:15	5	19:9–10	8
20:16	5, 97	19:10	23
20:17	5, 105–107, 112	19:11	92
21	68	19:12	23
21:15	67	19:13–14	8
21:16	92	19:17–18	8
21:17	67	19:18	7, 23, 108
22:16–17	84	19:34	23
23:4	92	19:35–36	92
24	35	20:10	82
24:9–11	34	20:20–21	83
24:12–31:18	34	23:15–16	63
25:16	10, 33	**Numbers**	
25:21	10	10–25	23
29:42–46	23	10:11–36:13	23
31:12–14	60	32:23	53
31:18	33	35:11	74
32–34	23	35:12	75
33:12–23	23	**Deuteronomy**	
		1:1–34:12	23
		4:1	22

Scripture Index

4:1–8	23
4:11–13	1–2
4:13	3, 33
4:24	38
4:37	23
4:44–28	23
5	2, 67
5:2–3	60
5:6–21	3
5:9	38
5:16	67
5:21	105
5:22	10
5:33	23
6	66
6:5	23, 66
6:6–9	67
7:7–9	23
7:9	23
7:13	23
9:4	24
9:9	32
9:10	10
9:10–17	33
10:2	10
10:4	3
10:5	10
10:10–15	22
10:12	23
10:14	95
10:17–18	23
10:18	23
10:18–19	23
11:1	23
11:13	23–24
12–26	3
18:5	51
18:7	51
19:9	23–24
19:14	92
20:5	75
21:18–21	67
21:20	68
22:23–24	82
22:24	84
23:2	83
23:5	23
26:4–11	23
26:16–19	23
28:10	50
29:17	23
30:6	23
30:11	24
30:11–16	24
30:16	24
32:46–47	23
34:28	32

Joshua

6:16–17	110
7	110
7:21	110

Judges

2:2–3	44
10:6	45
10:11	45

1 Kings

8:9	10
11:1–8	38
11:4	38

Nehemiah

9:13–14	60

Job

Scripture Index

42:1–6	55	2:2	38
Psalms		4:2	11, 82
1:1–2	22	4:11–14	85–86
7:17	51	**Joel**	
19:10	113	2:32	51
20:7	51	**Micah**	
51	98	4:5	51
51:5	98	**Zephaniah**	
58	100	3:12	51
58:3	99, 103	**Malachi**	
66:2	51	2:5	51
89:3	51	3:8–9	93, 96
102:15	51		
113:2	51	**New Testament**	
116:4	51	**Matthew**	
119:1–176	22	5:1–12	76
Proverbs		5:21	76
6:20–23	68	5:21–24	73
6:23	68	5:27–30	82
13:15	53	5:33–37	87
23:22	68	5:37	97, 100
23:24–25	68	5:39	77
Isaiah		6:24	108
20:13	52	6:33	96
49:6	23	7:1–6	54
50:10	51	7:12	6–7, 55, 95
56:6	51		
59:19	51	7:21–23	55, 87
Jeremiah		12:36–37	87
5:7	85	15	68
7:9	11, 82	15:5	69
14:13–16	52	15:6	69
14:16	54	15:7–9	52
17:9	92	15:8–9	55
Hosea		19:4–6	86
1:2	37	19:16–19	94

Scripture Index

19:17	33
19:18	11
20:28	22
21:12–13	77
22:37	39
22:37–40	1, 7, 36, 39
22:39	108
23:23	7
26:39	53
26:42	53

Mark

7	22
7:10	9
10:19	11

Luke

10:30	78
10:37	79
12:13–21	109
12:15	109
12:20	109
18:9–14	53
18:20	11

John

1:14	23
3:16	56
8:1–11	82
19:26–27	69
19:36	22

Acts

2	35
8:32–35	22
17:28	56
20:7	62
23:1–5	56

Romans

1:24–25	45
5:8	24, 56
7:1–7	22
7:12–14	22–23
8:3	22
8:28	24
8:32	22
11:22	53
13:7	94
13:8	24
13:8–10	9
13:9	11
13:10	24

1 Corinthians

2:9	24
3:16–17	23
5:7	22
6:9–10	93
8:3	24
10:26	96
16:2	62

2 Corinthians

3	22
5:21	22
10:5	95

Galatians

2:20	24
3–4	22–23
5:14	9, 24
6:1–2	55
6:7	53

Ephesians

2:4	24
2:14–15	61
3:5	110
4:15	55

Scripture Index

4:26	77	13:4	87
4:28	90, 95	13:5	96
4:29	52	**James**	
5:4	52	1:5–8	53
5:5	108, 110	1:13	110
5:22–33	86	1:13–15	110
6:1–3	65, 67	1:14–15	110
6:1–4	9, 70	2:8	9, 24
Philippians		2:8–13	9
1:21	111	3:16	95
2:3–4	111	4:1–6	53
2:3–11	95	4:13–17	53
3:3–8	111	4:15	55
4:6–7	111	5:19–20	55
Colossians		**1 Peter**	
1:16	48	1:15–16	19
2:14–17	61	2:9	18
3:5	108	2:9–10	39
3:8–10	101	2:22	22
1 Thessalonians		4:11	55
4:9	24	**1 John**	
1 Timothy		1:7	22
1:8	22–23	2:2	22
6:19–20	111	2:16	106
2 Timothy		3:17	7
3:16	21–23	4:10–11	24
Titus		4:12	20
1:10–16	53	4:18	18
1:16	55	4:20	7
3:9	22	4:20–21	20
Hebrews		5:2–3	24
7–10	22–23	5:3	24
8:6	62	**Revelation**	
8:6–13	61–62	1:10	62
9:4	10	21:8	102–103
12:24	62	21:27	104

Scripture Index

22:18–19   55

CREDITS

Select Scripture quotations are taken from the NEW AMERICAN STANDARD BIBLE®, copyright© 1960, 1962, 1963, 1968, 1971, 1972, 1973, 1975, 1977, 1995 by The Lockman Foundation. Used by permission.

Select Scripture quotations are taken from the NEW KING JAMES VERSION®. Copyright© 1982 by Thomas Nelson, Inc. Used by permission. All rights reserved.

Select Scripture quotations are taken from the NEW REVISED STANDARD VERSION BIBLE, copyright © 1989 National Council of the Churches of Christ in the United States of America. Used by permission. All rights reserved worldwide.

Select Scriptures quotations are taken from the Holy Bible, New International Version®, NIV®. Copyright © 1973, 1978, 1984, 2011 by Biblica, Inc.™ Used by permis-

Credits

sion of Zondervan. All rights reserved worldwide. www.zondervan.com The "NIV" and "New International Version" are trademarks registered in the United States Patent and Trademark Office by Biblica, Inc.®

Scripture quotations marked HCSB are been taken from the Holman Christian Standard Bible®, Copyright © 1999, 2000, 2002, 2003 by Holman Bible Publishers. Used by permission. Holman Christian Standard Bible®, Holman CSB®, and HCSB® are federally registered trademarks of Holman Bible Publishers.

Scripture quotations from The Authorized (King James) Version. Rights in the Authorized Version in the United Kingdom are vested in the Crown. Reproduced by permission of the Crown's patentee, Cambridge University Press.

Scripture quotations are from the ESV® Bible (The Holy Bible, English Standard Version®), copyright © 2001 by Crossway, a publishing ministry of Good News Publishers. Used by permission. All rights reserved

CONTRIBUTORS

Bill Bagents (DMin Amridge University) is Professor of Ministry, Counseling and Biblical Studies at Heritage Christian University.

Jeremy Barrier (PhD Brite Divinity School, Texas Christian University) is Professor of Biblical Literature at Heritage Christian University.

W. Kirk Brothers (PhD Southern Baptist Theological Seminary) is President of Heritage Christian University.

Nathan Daily (PhD Claremont Graduate University) is Heritage Christian University Registrar and Assistant Professor of Religion.

Arvy Dupuy (MA Amridge University) is Adjunct Instructor at Heritage Christian University.

Ed Gallagher (PhD Hebrew Union College) is Professor of Christian Scripture at Heritage Christian University.

Philip Goad (BA Heritage Christian University) preaches for North Highlands Church of Christ in Russellville, Alabama and serves as Director of Alumni Relations at Heritage Christian University.

Justin Guin (MDiv Freed-Hardeman University) is Adjunct Instructor at Heritage Christian University as serves as Youth Minister with the Double Springs Church of Christ in Double Springs, Alabama.

Travis Harmon (MMin Heritage Christian University) is Vice President of Student Services and Instructor of Ministry at Heritage Christian University.

Matt Heupel (MMin Freed-Hardeman University) is Adjunct Instructor at Heritage Christian University and preaches for the Woodlawn Church of Christ in Florence, Alabama.

Michael Jackson (EdD Union University) is Vice President for Academic Affairs and Associate Professor of Education and New Testament at Heritage Christian University.

C. Wayne Kilpatrick (MAR Harding School of Theology) is Emeritus Professor of Church History at Heritage Christian University.

Brad McKinnon (PhD in progress Aberdeen University) is Associate Professor and Director of Field Education at Heritage Christian University.

BEREAN STUDY SERIES

The Ekklesia of Christ (2015)

What Real Christianity Looks Like (2016)

Clothed in Christ (2017)

Instructions of Living (2018)

Visions of Grace (2019)

Cloud of Witnesses (2020)

For the Glory of God (2021)

Majesty and Mercy (2022)

To see full catalog of Heritage Christian University Press and its imprint Cypress Publications, visit www.hcu.edu/publications.

www.ingramcontent.com/pod-product-compliance
Lightning Source LLC
Chambersburg PA
CBHW071455070526
44578CB00001B/346